ALLELUIA

Easter
Crafts
and
Activities

Gospel Light

How to make clean copies from this book

Editorial Staff
Publisher, William T. Greig • **Senior Consulting Publisher,** Dr. Elmer L. Towns • **Publisher, Research, Planning and Development,** Billie Baptiste • **Managing Editor,** Lynnette Pennings, M.A. • **Senior Consulting Editors,** Dr. Gary S. Greig, Wesley Haystead, M.S.Ed. • **Senior Editor, Theological and Biblical Issues,** Bayard Taylor, M.Div. • **Editorial Team,** Elizabeth Lubaczewski, Linda Mattia, Jay Bea Summerfield • **Designer,** Carolyn Henderson

Contents

INTRODUCTION 6
TALKING ABOUT EASTER WITH
YOUNG CHILDREN 7

CRAFTS 9
Craft Tips 10

Early Childhood

Praise Tambourines 13
Place Mats 14
Egg-Carton Caterpillar 15
Easter Tree 16
Springtime Butterfly 18
Pop-Up Flower 20
Picture Poem 22
Butterfly Card 24
Life-Sized Drawings 25
Crayon Posters 26
Praise Shakers 27
Easter Badges 28
Paint-Drop Butterflies 30
The Road to Jerusalem 31
Promise Kite 32

Lower Elementary

Easter Windows 33
Praise Palms 34
Cardboard-Tube Butterfly 36
"He Lives!" Pencil Toppers 38
Easter Praise Chain 40
Sign Language Pictures 41
Easter Banners 42
"Jesus Is Alive!" Picture Frame 43
"He Is Risen" Shadow Box 44
Palm Sunday Mural 46
Puppet Theater 47
Easter Surprise Packages 48
Easter Buddies 49

Upper Elementary

Clothespin Cross 50
Easter Poster 51
Clothespin Planter 52

Bible Covers .53

Quilled Message 54

Easter Cards Service Project 55

Painted Flowerpot 56

Linoleum Mosaic 57

Bread Sculptor 58

"I'm a Believer!" Fish 59

GAMES 61

Game Tips 62

Lower Elementary

Discover the Reason 63

An Eggs-tra Puzzling Hunt! 64

The Gift of Easter 65

Follow That Friend! 66

Verse Circles .67

Glad Tag 68

Guess Who 69

Go Fish! 70

Upper Elementary

Hidden Messages 72

Sentence, Anyone? 73

Host a Hunt .74

Answer Match 75

Matching Dots 76

ACTIVITIES 77

Activity Tips .78

Early Childhood

Bean Sprouts .79

Flower Surprises 80

Scent Sense 81

Going Shopping 82

Rhythm Instruments 83

Blocks Road 84

Mirror Talk 85

Welcome the King 86

Build a Town .87

Real or Unreal? 88

Walk the Path 89

Follow Me 90

Finger Plays 91

Activity and Coloring Pages 97

Lower Elementary

Extra! Extra! .139

Praise Parade! 140

Easter Outreach Tree 141

Touch and Feel Pictures 142

Singing Praise 143

Praise Puzzles 144

Find the Match .147

Easter Reminder 148

Upper Elementary

Who Saw Him? .150

Easter Traditions 151

Weighing Your Wealth 152

Easter Grace 153

Whatzit Mean? 154

The Hope of Easter 157

Getting Your Hopes Up 158

Praise King Jesus 159

Where'd It Go? 160

Egg-Carton Holy Week 161

Krazy Kapers 162

Word Connections 165

He's Alive! 166

Going Fishing 170

I Will Return 173

STORIES .177
Story Tips 178

An Exciting Day in Jerusalem (Palm Sunday) . .179

The Saddest Day (Good Friday) 181

The Gladdest Day (Easter) 183

The Best News! (Ascension) 185

The First Easter .187

SNACKS .191
Snack Tips 192

Popcorn Mix 194

Spring Punch 195

Peanut Butter Banana Balls 196

Popcorn Shapes .197

Fruit Pizza 198

Animal Cutout Sandwiches 199

Matzos and Hard-Boiled Eggs 200

Cinnamon Yogurt 201

Pita Bread 202

Nana 'n' Cookie Pudding 203

Soft Pretzels 204

Chow Mein Chewies 205

Fresh Fruit with Coconut Dip 206

Australian Lamingtons 207

Introduction

Is the true joy of the Easter celebration getting lost among excited talk of bunnies, candy and coloring eggs? While sharing the enthusiasm for celebrating Easter with your children, here's the help you need to bring the true focus of Easter back to the forefront—ideas for sharing special times with your child, for providing unique experiences for your child and his or her friends, or for supplementing or creating special programs for Easter churchtime, for a kids' club or for a homeschool setting.

How to Get the Most Out of This Book

First, look through all the sections ("Crafts," "Games," "Activities," "Stories" and "Snacks") to acquaint yourself with all the ideas you now have at your fingertips.

- Each section begins with helpful tips to make your efforts in that area easier and more effective.
- Each craft, game and activity is labeled with the appropriate age level and contains a complete list of needed materials. Many of them include conversation guides to help you share the true message of Easter with children.
- Each of the four installments of the Easter story is complete with discussion questions, a Bible memory verse and a short prayer. A complete retelling of all the events in one story is also provided.
- Delicious, easy-to-prepare snacks round out the resources assembled for you.

If you are leading a large group of children, be sure to plan your program and choose your activities well in advance. That will give you time to recruit any helpers and gather the materials you'll need.

Schedule Options

Early Childhood (Ages 2-5)
60 minutes
Activities (2 or 3): 30 minutes
Bible Story: 5 minutes
Snack: 10 minutes
Craft: 15 minutes

90 minutes
Activities (3 or 4): 40 minutes
Bible Story: 5 minutes
Free Play: 20 minutes
Snack: 10 minutes
Craft: 15 minutes

Elementary (Grades 1-6)
60 minutes
Activity: 15 minutes
Bible Story: 15 minutes
Game or Snack: 15 minutes
Craft: 15 minutes

90 minutes
Activity: 20 minutes
Bible Story: 20 minutes
Game or Snack: 20 minutes
Craft: 30 minutes

Once you have these basics in hand, start with those things designated for your child's age group, but don't ignore the possibility of adapting something from an older or younger age level to fit your needs. Also keep in mind that with a little thought, substitutions can be made for materials that you may not have on hand. We hope you will be inspired to add your own creative ideas.

Have a joyful Easter—and may God bless your endeavors with kids!

Talking About Easter with Young Children

Three-year-old Alan thought he had Easter analyzed. Confidently he explained, "It was when Jesus arose from the grave and the Easter bunny hopped out after Him!"

Easter is a joyful time, but it can also be a time of confusion for children as they get the secular and biblical aspects of the Easter celebration confused. Easter baskets, eggs and bunnies sometimes overshadow the true and beautiful Easter story from God's Word.

Jesus Is Alive!

"We are happy at Easter because Jesus is alive!" is what children need to hear from you often at Eastertime. Spring flowers, happy music, brightly colored eggs, gifts, even new clothes can all be part of Easter celebrations; help children understand that all of these things can be used to show and share joy because Jesus is living.

Long after Easter Day is past, the biblical truth that Jesus is alive is what children need to remember.

Keep It Simple

As adults, we need to keep in mind that words and phrases that are quite clear to us often have clouded meanings for young children. For example, "Jesus died and rose again" is not likely to have meaning or seem like a happy statement to little children.

Children have very vague and uneasy notions about what death involves. They usually see it as some kind of sad separation. Avoid dwelling on the gruesome aspects of the Crucifixion that may emotionally overwhelm young children.

Instead of dwelling on the details of Christ's death, help children grasp the great truth of the Easter story—a living Savior. You can help them understand by talking about the way Jesus' friends must have felt:

"Jesus' friends were very sad when Jesus died. Some of them even cried because they thought they would never see Jesus again. They were very happy when they found out that Jesus did not stay dead. They must have laughed and hugged each other. They told all their friends, 'Jesus isn't dead. He is alive! Jesus is living.'"

As you talk about the first Easter, show appropriate pictures from children's Bibles or Bible storybooks. Talking with children about the pictures will give you opportunities to observe what is most important to them, clarify any misconceptions and build positive feelings about the Easter story.

As a child's ability to understand increases, so does his or her curiosity. As they hear about the first Easter, children may have several questions. The following suggestions will help you give meaningful answers they can accept and understand.

Why did they kill Jesus?

Jesus was hurt and killed by people who did not like Him. They did not know that God sent Jesus to love and help everyone. But God made Jesus alive again. Jesus is living! (See Matthew 27:11—28:6.)

Where is Jesus?

He is living in heaven now with God, His Father. And everything is very beautiful in heaven. And everyone is very happy there. (See Ephesians 1:20 and Colossians 3:1.)

What is Jesus doing in heaven?

Jesus told us He is making a wonderful home in heaven. All who love Him (everyone in God's family) will be with Him in heaven someday. (See John 14:1-7.)

What is it like in heaven?

The Bible tells us that heaven is more beautiful than we can ever think. No one gets sick or hurt there. There is no sadness—only happiness! There are no tears—only happy faces and singing voices. (See Revelation 21.)

Will Jesus come again to earth?

Yes! But only God knows when it will be—some wonderful day! Everyone who loves Jesus (everyone in God's family) will be glad to see Him and to go with Him to the heavenly home He has made. (See 1 Thessalonians 4:14—5:10 and Acts 1:9-11.)

(This and other helpful articles for parents and teachers can be found in the reproducible *Sunday School Smart Pages* from Gospel Light.)

ALLELUIA!

Crafts

Craft Tips

Few things spark a child's imagination like working with a craft. When children are cutting, gluing, pasting, drawing or shaping, they are using their imaginations to picture and better understand a truth or an idea. While they are working, different parts of their minds are engaged in thinking and understanding.

What can you do to make sure each craft is successful and fun for children?

- Encourage creativity in each child! Remember that the process of creating is more important than the final product.

- Choose projects that are appropriate for the skill level of the children you are dealing with.

- Show an interest in the unique way each child approaches a project. Treat each child's product as a "masterpiece!"

To help children successfully complete some of the activities suggested in this book, a few basic skills are required. These skills—folding, taping, cutting and gluing—must be learned. As you know, not all children learn at the same rate or by the same means. Some of the various ways to help children learn to succeed at these four tasks are given here.

Folding

1. Prefold paper as needed; then open it back up. Paper will then fold easily along the prefolded lines when child refolds it.

2. Before giving paper to child, score the line to be folded by placing a ruler on the line. Then draw a ballpoint pen with no ink in it along the ruler's edge. The line will fold easily into place.

3. Hold the corners of the paper in position to be folded. Tell the child to "press and rub" where he or she wants to fold it.

Taping

1. An easy solution for the problems of taping is to use double-sided tape whenever appropriate. Lay the tape down on the paper where it is needed. Child attaches the item that needs to be taped.

2. If double-sided tape is not available or is not appropriate, place a piece of tape lightly on the page where it is needed. Child rubs on tape to attach it securely to paper.

Cutting

1. Cutting with scissors is one of the most difficult tasks for any young child to master.

Consider purchasing "training scissors" (available at educational supply stores) to assist in teaching a child how to cut.

2. If you have a large group of children, have available two or three pairs of left-handed scissors (also available at educational supply stores). All scissors should be approximately 4 inches (10 cm) long and should have blunt ends.

3. Hold paper tightly at ends or sides while child cuts.

4. Begin to cut paper for child to follow. Child follows cut you have begun.

5. Draw simple lines outside actual cut lines for the child to follow. This will help a child cut close to the desired shape—though it will not be exact.

6. Provide scrap paper for child to practice cutting.

Gluing

1. Have child use a glue bottle to apply a spot of glue to a large sheet of paper; then he or she presses a smaller piece of paper onto glued area.

2. Provide a glue stick (available at variety stores) for the child to use. Take off cap and roll up glue for child. Child "colors" with glue stick over desired area.

3. Pour glue into a shallow container. Thin slightly by adding a small amount of water. Child uses paintbrush to spread glue over desired area. This idea works well when a large surface needs to be glued.

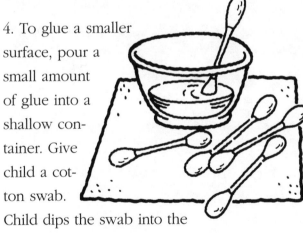

4. To glue a smaller surface, pour a small amount of glue into a shallow container. Give child a cotton swab. Child dips the swab into the glue and rubs on desired area.

5. When using glue bottles, buy the smallest bottles for children to use. Refill small bottles from a large bottle. Adjust the top of each bottle to limit amount of glue that comes out. Instruct child to put "tiny dots of glue" on paper. Clean off and tightly close top of each bottle when finished.

Remember not to expect perfection. Accept all attempts at accomplishing the task. Specific and honest praise will encourage the child to attempt the task again!

(These and other helpful hints for parents and teachers can be found in the reproducible *Sunday School Smart Pages* from Gospel Light.)

Praise Tambourines

Materials: Hole punch, one foil pie plate or paper plate and four jingle bells for each child, scissors, ruler, several colors of crepe paper, chenille wires, tape.

Preparation: Punch four holes in each plate (see sketch). Cut crepe paper into lengths about 12 inches (30 cm) long, one for each child. Cut chenille wires into 4-inch (10-cm) lengths.

Procedure: Child uses chenille wires to fasten bells loosely to plate and then selects a colored crepe-paper streamer and tapes it to the tambourine. Child plays tambourine by tapping fingers in center or by shaking it. Talk about ways to praise the Lord.

What kind of sound does your tambourine make? Let children respond. **I think tambourines make a happy sound. And I feel like making happy sounds when I think about Jesus' love for us. Our Bible tells about people who made happy sounds when they saw Jesus. They said, "Hosanna! Hosanna!" That's like saying "Praise the Lord! Praise the Lord!" Today we can praise the Lord with our tambourines.**

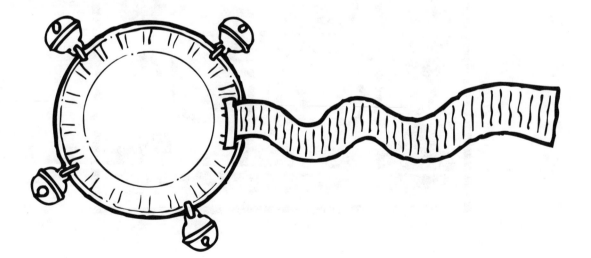

Place Mats

Materials: Crayons or markers, one large sheet of construction paper for each child, a variety of materials for decorations (flower stickers, doilies, rickrack, yarn), scissors, glue; optional—clear Con-Tact paper.

Preparation: Letter "Jesus is alive!" on each sheet of paper.

Procedure: As you talk about Jesus' resurrection, have children decorate place mats using materials provided. (Optional: Cover finished place mats with clear Con-Tact paper.) Encourage children to use place mats to tell family members that Jesus is alive.

Our Bible tells us that Jesus has risen. Another way to say that is "Jesus is alive!" Those are the words on your place mat. We are glad that Jesus is alive!

Egg-Carton Caterpillar

Materials: Scissors, cardboard egg-carton bottoms, awl, wide-tip markers, chenille wires, gummed hole reinforcements; optional—newspaper, tempera paint, water, shallow containers, paint smocks or old shirts, paintbrushes.

Preparation: Cut carton bottoms in half lengthwise, one length for each child (see sketch a). Use awl to punch holes in first section of each carton length (see sketch b). (Optional: Cover work area with newspaper. Put paint and water in separate containers.)

Procedure: Child colors carton length with markers. (Optional: Children put on smocks or shirts and paint their carton lengths.) Help each child insert a chenille wire through punched holes and bend wire for antennas (see sketch c). Child then glues hole reinforcements for eyes. Arrange a caterpillar parade. **Caterpillars are fun to watch! When we see them crawling on the ground, we know spring is finally here! Springtime is when we celebrate that Jesus died and is alive again. We're glad for springtime and we're glad that Jesus is alive!**

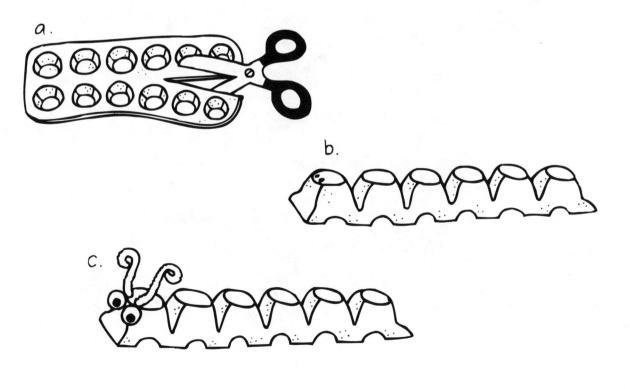

Easter Tree

Materials: Easter Tree Patterns, poster board, pencils, scissors, indoor tree or flowering branch in vase of water, ruler, narrow ribbon, paper, markers or crayons, hole punch.

Preparation: Trace Easter Tree Patterns onto poster board and cut out several copies of each design for children to use as patterns. (For younger children, cut out several shapes for each child.) Place indoor tree or vase with branch in it in an accessible spot. Cut ribbon into 6-inch (15-cm) lengths.

Procedure: Let's celebrate Easter by deco-rating an Easter tree! Use the patterns to help children think of things that remind them of Easter. Older children make decorations by tracing patterns onto paper, cutting them out and decorating them with markers or crayons. Younger children simply decorate the shapes with markers or crayons. Punch holes near the top of shapes. Children thread ribbon through holes and hang decorations on the indoor tree or the flowering branch. **All the decorations on our Easter tree help us remember that Jesus died for us and is alive again!**

Springtime Butterfly

Materials: Springtime Butterfly Pattern, photocopier, paper, glue, scissors, a variety of decorating materials (crayons, markers, glitter glue, small pieces of construction paper or tissue paper, etc.).

Preparation: Photocopy a pattern for each child.

Procedure: Talk about the many signs of new life that are seen during springtime—plants, baby birds, butterflies, etc. Then give each child a Springtime Butterfly Pattern. Set out glue, scissors and decorating materials. Children select materials and decorate their butterflies. **We are glad to see all the signs of new life in the springtime. We are glad Jesus is alive and that He loves us!**

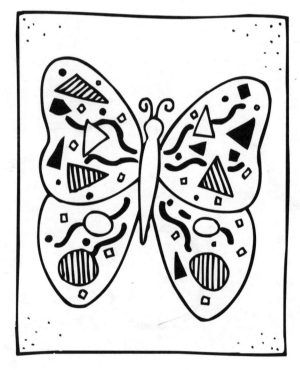

Pop-Up Flower

Materials: Pop-Up Flower Patterns, pencil, construction paper, scissors, awl, one small Styrofoam cup and one plastic straw or unsharpened pencil for each child, crayons or markers, tape.

Preparation: Trace Pop-Up Flower Patterns onto construction paper and cut out one flower and one set of leaves for each child. Use awl (or scissors) to make one hole centered in the bottom of each cup (hole must be large enough for straw or pencil to slip through it).

Procedure: Child colors flower and leaves and then tapes them to straw or pencil (see sketch). Have each child insert straw or pencil in hole in cup bottom. **Pull your flower down into the cup and it's like wintertime, when the flowers are sleeping. Slowly push up your flower and it's like springtime, when the flowers start to grow and bloom! We're happy to see flowers in the springtime. We're also happy that Jesus died for us and is alive again!**

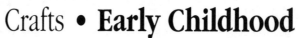

Picture Poem

Materials: Picture Poem Pattern, photocopier, paper, scissors, crayons or markers, stapler and staples or thinned glue in shallow container and glue brushes, one 9×12-inch (22.5×30-cm) sheet of construction paper for each child.

Preparation: Photocopy one Picture Poem Pattern for each child. Trim page where indicated.

Procedure: Child uses crayons or markers to color pictures and border around poem and then staples or glues poem to construction paper. As children work, say the poem aloud several times. **Do you know why we're glad at Easter? We're glad because Jesus is living.** Read the poem aloud, encouraging the children to "read" along with you. **You can use this poem to decorate your room and to remind yourself of what makes Easter a special day.**

Jesus is living!
He's living today!
That's the good news
Of glad Easter Day!

Cut along this line.

Jesus is living!

He's living today!

That's the good news

Of glad Easter Day!

Butterfly Card

Materials: Scissors, ruler, brightly colored tissue paper, one sheet of 9×12-inch (22.5×30-cm) construction paper and two 6-inch (15-cm) chenille wires for each child, marker, tape.

Preparation: Cut two 5-inch (12.5-cm) squares of tissue paper for each child. Fold construction paper in half. Add lettering to inside of each card as shown in Sketch a.

Procedure: For each butterfly, assist child to bend chenille wire in half. Child gathers tissue paper in center and lays it inside wire.

Help child twist wire ends together to enclose tissue paper and form antennas (see sketch b). Each child makes two butterflies and tapes them to front of card (see sketch c). **What pretty colors did you use for your butterflies? Your butterflies look like they're ready to fly away! We're glad for butterflies. And we're glad Jesus is living! You can share this good news by giving someone the pretty card you made. Who are you going to give your card to?**

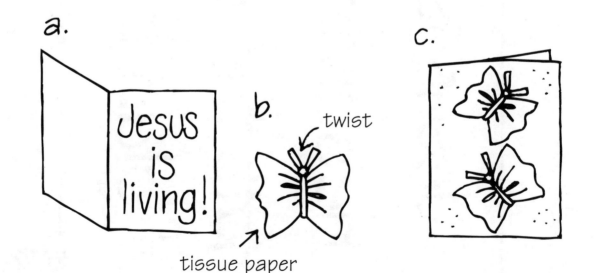

a.

Jesus is living!

b.

twist

tissue paper

c.

Life-Sized Drawings

Materials: Scissors, measuring stick, roll of newsprint or butcher or shelf paper, crayons, tape.

Preparation: Cut a 4-foot (1.2-m) length of paper for each child.

Procedure: Lay paper on floor. Each child takes a turn to lie down on a piece of paper while you draw around his or her body with a dark crayon. Tape papers to wall. Child colors his or her outline. Talk with children about things they like to do and places they like to go. Emphasize Jesus' promise to be with them always.

Look how big you are growing! Now that you're bigger, what do you like to do at Eastertime? Let children respond. **At Eastertime we celebrate that Jesus died and lives again. Just before Jesus went back to heaven He said, "I am with you always." We're so glad that Jesus is with us everywhere we go.** Encourage interested children to say a thank-you prayer to Jesus.

Easter Crafts and Activities 25

Crayon Posters

Materials: Newspaper, white crayon, white construction paper, tempera paint, shallow containers, water, paint smocks or old shirts, paintbrushes.

Preparation: Cover work area with newspaper. On each sheet of construction paper, use white crayon to draw a happy face and letter the words "Jesus loves me." Press hard with crayon so that there is a large buildup of crayon wax. Pour a small amount of paint into each shallow container and then add water to make the paint very thin.

Procedure: Wearing paint smocks or shirts, children paint over white construction paper you prepared. The crayon will resist the paint and the happy faces and messages will appear. Talk with children about Jesus' love. **Were you surprised when you saw the happy face on your paper? Many of Jesus' friends were surprised when Jesus died and came back to life. They were happy to know that Jesus is alive, and we are, too!**

Praise Shakers

Materials: One paper plate for each child, tape or stapler and staples, crayons or felt pens, macaroni or dried beans, spoons, cassette/CD of children's Christian music, cassette/CD player.

Preparation: Fold in half and tape or staple each paper plate, leaving enough room for children to insert macaroni or dried beans (see sketch a).

Procedure: Children color plates and then spoon in a small amount of macaroni or dried beans. Assist children in taping or stapling shakers closed (see sketch b). Lead children in using the shakers as they listen to or sing along with music on the cassette/CD.

Our Bible tells us to sing praises to the Lord. When we sing praises to the Lord, it means we thank the Lord for the good things He has done for us. We sing praises because Jesus died for us and is alive again! We can use our voices and our shakers to make happy praise sounds.

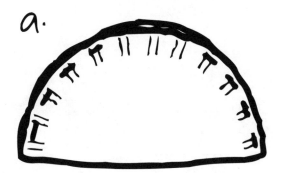

Easter Crafts and Activities

Easter Badges

Materials: Bible, Easter Badge Pattern, photocopier, paper, felt pens, scissors, yarn, stapler and staples, tape.

Preparation: Photocopy one Easter Badge Pattern for each child.

Procedure: Child uses felt pens to color badge. Letter name on badge where indicated. Cut a long length of yarn and staple it securely to the back of the page as shown in Sketch a. Child folds page over, tapes closed as shown in Sketch b and then wears badge around neck, turning badge over to show the good news.

Why do you think Easter is a special day for people who love Jesus? Listen carefully to children's comments. **Jesus is alive! And that good news is right here on your badge.** Read the badge to child. **You can read these words on your badge to your family. Then they will know why Easter is such a happy day, too!** As children work, read aloud the words on the badge. Soon children will be saying the words with you. Then open your Bible. **We've been saying the good news together that Jesus is alive. Our Bible says it this way, "It is true! The Lord has risen."**

a.

b.

← tape

child's name

has happy news to tell.

Jesus is alive!

Paint-Drop Butterflies

Materials: Felt pen, one sheet of white or light-colored construction paper for each child, newspaper, scissors, paint smocks or old shirts, tempera paint in primary colors, shallow containers, eyedroppers.

Preparation: Fold sheets of paper in half and on each draw lines as shown in Sketch a. Cover work area with newspaper. Pour each paint color into a separate container.

Procedure: Child cuts on lines and then unfolds papers to reveal butterfly shape (see sketch b). After putting on smock or shirt, child drops paint from eyedroppers onto one half of paper. Child refolds paper, pressing to spread paint. Child unfolds to see design on butterfly's wings (see sketch c).

I see you are using red for your butterfly. How can you tell which color is red and which color is yellow? We can thank God for making your eyes to see colors. If child is interested, pray briefly, thanking God for his or her eyes. **The Bible tells us about a man named Thomas who didn't think Jesus was really alive UNTIL he saw Jesus with his own eyes. When Thomas saw Jesus, he knew Jesus is alive. I'm glad Jesus is alive!**

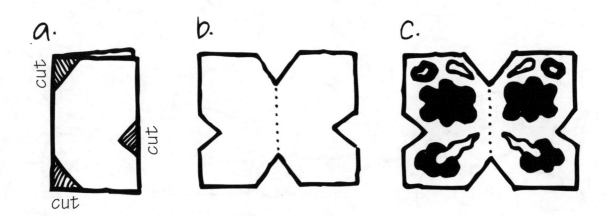

The Road to Jerusalem

Materials: Bible, scissors, measuring stick, butcher paper, tape, wide-tip felt pen, glue, shallow containers, green construction paper, fabric scraps, crayons, brushes; optional—sand, green leaves.

Preparation: Cut a 4-foot (1.2-m) length of butcher paper. Lay paper on a table, taping to secure. Outline a road on the paper with felt pen. Add several curves. Pour glue into shallow containers. Review the story of the first Palm Sunday (see Matthew 21:1-11).

Procedure: Briefly tell how people laid down palm branches and clothing to praise Jesus when He rode into Jerusalem on Palm Sunday. **The people wanted to show Jesus they knew how very important He was.**

Point to green paper. **We can tear this paper and make pretend branches to lay on the road for Jesus.** Point to fabric scraps. **We can pretend these are the coats people laid out on the road for Jesus.**

Children tear green paper to represent palm branches, cut fabric into smaller scraps to represent coats and then make a mural of the road to Jerusalem. Children color road with crayons and then brush glue on an area of the road and press "branches" and "coats" to road. (Optional: Children glue sand to road and then glue leaves to road for palm branches.)

Promise Kite

Materials: Paper cutter, construction paper and crepe paper in several colors, scissors, measuring stick, yarn or string, crayons or felt pens, staples and stapler.

Preparation: Use paper cutter or scissors to cut one construction paper kite shape for each child (see sketch a). Cut a 3-foot (.9-m) length of crepe paper and of yarn or string for each child.

Procedure: Child selects color of kite, decorates kite with crayons or felt pens, staples crepe paper to one end of kite for tail and staples yarn or string to other end (see sketch b).

Have you ever watched a real kite fly? What does it do? Sometimes it goes so far up in the sky, we can hardly see it. Our Bible tells about the time Jesus went back to heaven. He went up and up into the sky until the clouds hid Him and His friends couldn't see Him anymore. And even though we can't see Jesus, we know He's with us because He said He's always with us—and Jesus always keeps His promises!

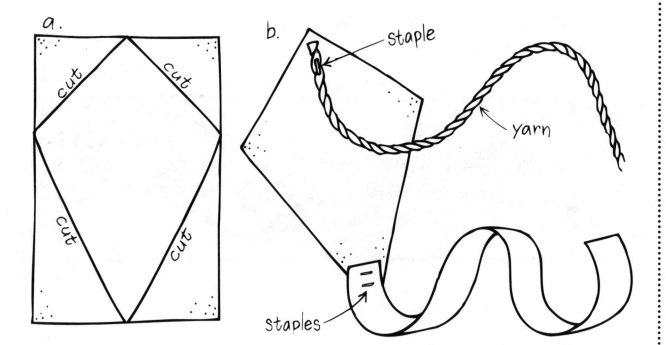

Easter Windows

Materials: Scissors, colored tissue paper, ruler, transparent tape.

Preparation: Cut tissue paper into pieces at least 4×6 inches (10×15 cm) in size, making at least two for each child. Cut one piece into a heart shape.

Procedure: Show heart shape you made. Tell children that at Easter, a heart shape is a reminder that Jesus loved us so much He died on the cross. Ask children to tell about shapes that remind them of Easter. Children may mention such ideas as a cross to remember that Jesus died, a rock to remember the tomb, a flower to remember the garden where Mary saw Jesus or a sun to remember the first Easter morning. Distribute tissue paper and scissors. Children cut out shapes and tape them onto windows (see sketch).

Praise Palms

Materials: Praise Palms Pattern, photocopier, paper, scissors, markers, hole punch, brass paper fasteners.

Preparation: Photocopy one Praise Palms Pattern for yourself and for each child. Make a sample set of branches, following the directions given below.

Procedure: Show sample Praise Palm and demonstrate how people waved branches in the air to honor Jesus on Palm Sunday.

Distribute Praise Palms Patterns. Have volunteers read the praise statements on the palms. Children cut out palm branches. Children may draw pictures on the backs of praise palms. Punch holes in the branches (on black dots) and use a paper fastener to hold together each child's set of branches. Let children wave palms as they sing along with or listen to an Easter song.

Crafts • Lower Elementary
Praise Palms Pattern

Jesus loves me.

Jesus forgives me.

Jesus is God's Son.

Jesus takes care of me.

Cardboard-Tube Butterfly

Materials: Construction paper in assorted colors (including black), Cardboard-Tube Butterfly Pattern, scissors, string, measuring stick, one cardboard tube approximately 5 inches (12.5cm) long and one chenille wire for each child, markers, glue, hole punch; optional—newspaper, paint, water, shallow containers, paint smocks or old shirts, paintbrushes.

Preparation: Set aside black construction paper. Fold other sheets of construction paper in half, place patterns on fold and cut one large and one small set of wings for each child. Cut one 36-inch (90-cm) length of string for each child. (Optional: Cover work area with newspaper. Pour paint and water into separate containers.)

Procedure: Instruct each child in the following procedures: Decorate the cardboard tube with markers. (Optional: Each child puts on a paint smock or old shirt and decorates the tube with paint.) Glue center section of the small set of wings to the center of the large set (see sketch a). Cut or tear small pieces of construction paper and glue them to the wings for decoration. Glue the center part of the large wings to the tube (see sketch b). Punch two circles from black construction paper and glue in place for eyes. Bend a chenille wire to make antennas for butterfly; glue to tube or push wire through cardboard to secure. Bend the top ends of wire into spirals. Punch hole in tube between antennas. Thread one end of string through hole and tie ends of string together to make a loop for hanging or holding

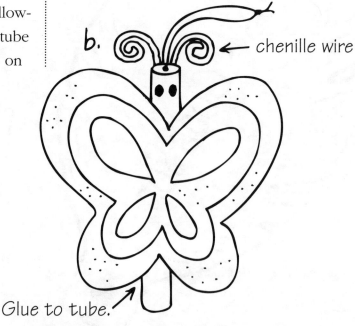

b. ← chenille wire

Glue to tube.

Glue small butterfly to large butterfly.

a.

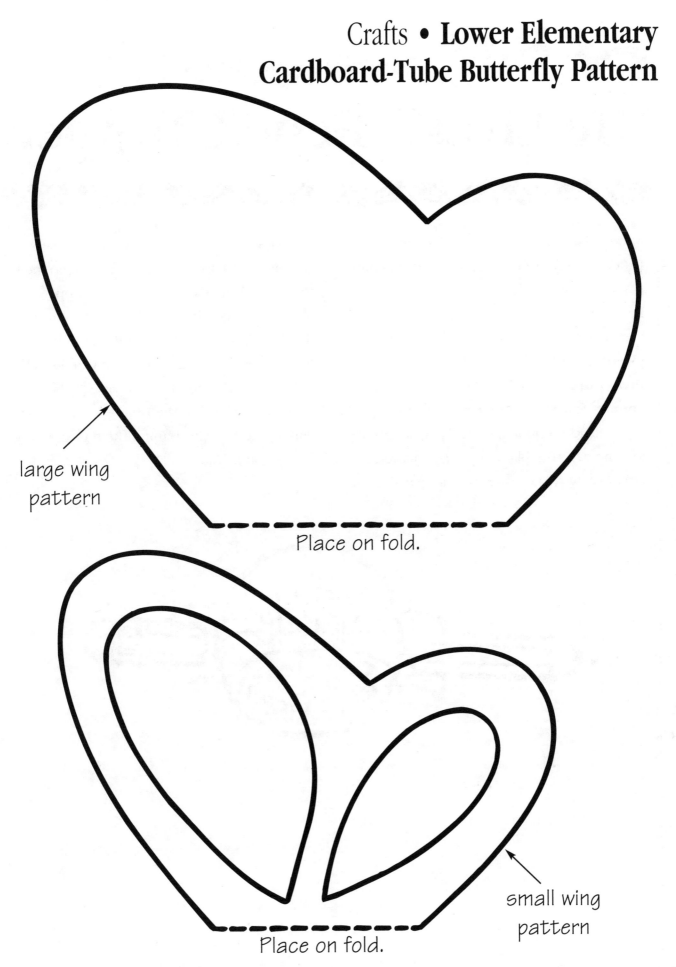

large wing
pattern

Place on fold.

small wing
pattern

Place on fold.

"He Lives!" Pencil Toppers

Materials: "He Lives!" Pencil Toppers Pattern and four new pencils for each child, markers, scissors, hole punch.

Preparation: Photocopy one pattern for each child. Make a sample pencil topper following directions given below.

Procedure: Distribute "He Lives!" Pencil Topper Patterns and four pencils to each child. Read the words on the pencil toppers together. On the blank toppers, children may either draw two of their favorite parts of the Easter story (for instance, Mary and Jesus, the empty tomb or the angel) or write their own Easter messages. When the toppers are completed, children cut them out, punch holes on the black dots on the tabs and slide pencils through the holes (see sketch). Encourage children to keep one of their pencils and to give the others to friends or family members to remind them of the good news about Jesus.

Jesus Is Alive!

He Is Risen!

He Lives!

Jesus Is My Savior!

Easter Praise Chain

Materials: Scissors, ruler, construction paper in a variety of colors, markers, eight small index cards, crayons, tape.

Preparation: Cut construction paper into 1×8-inch (2.5×20-cm) strips, two or three for each child. Letter one of these words on each small index card: "Easter," "Jesus," "alive," "disciples," "happy," "glad," "tomb," "angels."

Procedure: To breifly review the Easter story, place small index cards face down in one stack. Let volunteers choose a card and use the word on the card in a sentence that tells about Jesus and His death and resurrec-tion. Show children construction paper strips you have prepared and demonstrate how to make a paper chain. Distribute paper strips to children. On the strips, children write or draw the part of the Easter story that they want to praise God for. Assist children who need help writing.

As children complete their paper strips, guide them to make the paper chain by tap-ing the loops together with drawings and writing showing on the outside of the loops (see sketch). Display by attaching paper chain to wall, doorway or bulletin board.

Sign Language Pictures

Materials: Colored construction paper, pencils, scissors, glue, markers.

Preparation: From construction paper, cut two heart-shaped stencils large enough to fit around your spread hand.

Procedure: On paper, children trace around right hands with fingers spread and then cut out hand shapes. On paper of a contrasting color, children trace around heart stencils and then cut out heart shapes. Show children the sign for "I love you" (hold hand up as in sketch a). Children glue hands onto heart shapes, leaving the two middle fingers free. Demonstrate how to bend the two fingers forward and glue them to the palm to make the hand sign for "I love you" (see sketch a). Explain to children that we can show love to God at Easter with our words in prayers and songs; but even if we couldn't hear or speak, there are ways to show love to God. Be available to help children as they bend and glue the middle two fingers of their paper hands. Children may glue hearts onto sheets of construction paper and then write "I love You, Jesus" across the top of the paper (see sketch b).

a.

I love You, Jesus.

b.

Easter Banners

Materials: Hole punch, one large sheet of construction paper and a length of yarn for each child, picture Bible or Bible storybook with pictures of Easter story, scissors, markers, collage items (wrapping paper, ribbon, buttons, glitter, tissue paper, etc.), glue.

Preparation: Make a banner for each child by punching two holes and then tying yarn to make a hanger in each large sheet of construction paper (see sketch).

Procedure: Show Easter pictures from picture Bible or Bible storybook. Show a sheet of construction paper with a yarn hanger. Ask children to tell what words or pictures they would put on this banner to thank God for sending Jesus to die for us and live again. Children may suggest phrases like "Thank You, God" or "I'm glad Jesus is alive." Pass out banners, scissors, markers, collage items and glue. Children draw pictures or write words of thanks to God on the banners and then decorate banners by gluing collage items on them.

"Jesus Is Alive!" Picture Frame

Materials: Hole punch, one 9×12-inch (22.5×30-cm) sheet of lightweight poster board for each child, scissors, yarn, ruler, tape, marker, glue, 5×7-inch (12.5×17.5-cm) white paper, elbow macaroni, glitter.

Preparation: Punch two holes at the top of each poster board sheet. Cut yarn into 8-inch (20-cm) lengths. Wrap a piece of tape around one end of yarn to form "needle."

Letter "Jesus Is Alive!" on top of poster board sheets (see sketch a).

Procedure: Child draws favorite Easter scene on white paper and then glues picture onto poster board below lettering. Child decorates frame by gluing macaroni and glitter on edges. Help child draw yarn through holes, remove tape from yarn and tie yarn ends together to make a hanger (see sketch b).

"He Is Risen" Shadow Box

Materials: Scissors, two large sturdy paper plates for each child, Angel Picture, light-weight cardboard, hole punch, tempera paint (gray, brown and green), fine aquarium gravel or course sand (or bird grit), white glue, measuring cups and spoons, mixing bowl, shallow containers, newspaper, paint smocks or old shirts, paint-brushes, photocopier, paper, yarn, ruler, crayons, paper clips, paper fasteners; optional—dried flowers and greenery.

Day One

Preparation: Cut out center of plate, making hole slightly smaller than the size of Angel Picture (see sketch a)—one plate for each child. Cut cardboard into circles or stone shapes the same size as Angel Picture—one "stone" for each child. With hole punch, punch one hole close to the edge

of each cardboard stone. Make textured paint in bowl by mixing together 2 cups of gray paint, 1/2 cup of gravel or sand (or grit) and 4 tablespoons of white glue. Pour textured paint into shallow containers. Pour brown and green paint into shallow containers. Cover work area with newspaper.

Procedure: Have children put on paint smocks or old shirts. Children paint the underside of cut plate brown for a cave and green for grass (see sketch b). (Optional: Children may glue dried flowers and greenery onto grass portion of paper plate.) Children then paint one side of cardboard circle with gray textured paint. Let dry.

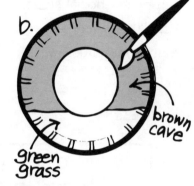

Day Two

Preparation: Photocopy one Angel Picture for each child. Cut one 6-inch (15-cm) length of yarn for each child.

Procedure: Children use crayons to color Angel Picture and then cut out picture and glue to front center of uncut plate. Then children punch two holes in the cutout paper plate as indicated in Sketch c and one hole at the top of uncut plate. Help children as needed to line up the holes at the tops of plates and glue the rims

"He Is Risen" Shadow Box

of plates together. The Angel Picture will show through the cutout paper plate. (Edges of plates should be paper-clipped together as shown in sketch c until glue has dried.) Help children attach the painted "stone" to the top paper plate with a paper fastener (see sketch d). Children then thread yarn through hole at top of plates and tie for a hanger.

Angel Picture

Palm Sunday Mural

Materials: Scissors, butcher paper, measuring stick, tape, children's Bible storybook with picture of Jesus riding a donkey into Jerusalem on Palm Sunday, crayons.

Preparation: Cut a long piece of butcher paper, allowing a 3-foot (.9-m) section of paper for each child. Tape butcher paper to a wall so that the bottom of the paper is even with the floor.

Procedure: Show Bible storybook picture. Briefly review the story, concentrating on what the people did to praise Jesus. (Sang songs. Waved palm branches. Shouted "Hosanna!" Placed palm branches and coats on the road.)

Children make a mural showing how they would praise Jesus if they had been in Jerusalem. Group children in pairs and distribute crayons. Children stand against the butcher paper and trace around each other (see sketch). Children draw facial features and Bible-times clothing details on their outlines. Letter "We Praise Jesus" at the top.

Why were the people in Jerusalem praising Jesus? (They were glad to see Him. He was famous because of His miracles. They wanted Him to be their leader.) **How can you praise Jesus? How has Jesus shown love to you? What good things has Jesus given you?**

Puppet Theater

Materials: Bible, three clothespins (not spring-type) or craft sticks and two sheets of construction paper for each child, markers, fabric scraps, scissors, glue; optional—books containing pictures of Bible-times clothing.

Preparation: Review the Bible story about the two disciples who met Jesus on the Road to Emmaus (Luke 24:13-35).

Procedure: Ask volunteers to tell the story about the two disciples who met Jesus on the road to Emmaus. Fill in any parts of the story the children don't remember or know. Distribute clothespins or craft sticks and construction paper. (Optional: Provide books containing pictures of Bible-times clothing.) Children use markers, fabric scraps, scissors and glue to create faces and clothing on the clothespins or sticks to represent the three characters (Jesus and the two disciples) in the Emmaus story (see sketch a).

Children draw a scene of the road to Emmaus on one sheet of construction paper and a Bible-times home on the other. Demonstrate how to fold and stand two sheets of construction paper back-to-back to use as a stage for the puppets to act out the events from the story (see sketch b). Encourage children to use their stages and puppets to retell the story to family members or friends.

a.

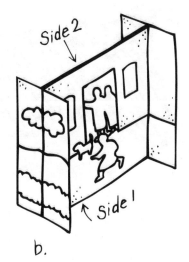

b.

Easter Surprise Packages

Materials: Markers, large sheet of paper, index cards, one toilet paper tube for each child, scissors, wrapping paper, tape, chenille wires; optional—stickers, individually wrapped candies, sticks of gum and/or other small gifts.

Preparation: Letter these sentences on large sheet of paper: "Jesus is alive!" and "Jesus is God's Son." Make a sample surprise package following the directions given below.

Procedure: Let volunteers open the sample package and read the sentences inside it. Show large sheet of paper and read sentences with children. Each child copies the sentences about Jesus onto an index card. Child rolls or folds the index card and places it in a paper tube. (Optional: Children also place stickers, candy, gum and/or other small gifts in the tube.) Help children as needed to cover tubes with wrapping paper, tape paper down and close ends with chenille wire twists (see sketch).

Ask each child to tell the name of a person to give the package to. Encourage children to think of people they know who may not know much about Jesus. Pray together that God will help the people who receive the surprise packages to learn about Jesus.

Easter Buddies

Materials: Pen, self-adhesive address labels, scissors, paper bag, 9×12-inch (22.5×30-cm) colored construction paper, markers, glue, glitter, ribbon, large envelopes; optional—stickers, sticks of gum, small candy hearts, confetti.

Preparation: Write each child's name and address on an address label. Cut labels apart and put them into paper bag.

Procedure: Talk about what it means to have a secret pal, or buddy. Give each child a sheet of construction paper. Ask volunteers to tell the events in the Easter story. Encourage children to draw pictures about these events for their "secret Easter buddy." Children may also glue glitter and pieces of ribbon to their pictures. Children put completed pictures inside envelopes. (Optional: Children put stickers, gum, candy hearts, and/or confetti inside their envelopes as surprises for their secret buddies.) Each child then secretly picks an address label from the paper bag and places it inside the envelope. During the week, put the address labels on the appropriate envelopes and mail them to the children.

Clothespin Cross

Materials: Five spring-type clothespins for each child, scissors, measuring stick, 1 1/2-inch (3.75-cm) ribbon, gold metallic thread, glue.

Preparation: Remove springs from clothespins. Cut one 15-inch (37.5-cm) length and one 9-inch (22.5-cm) length of ribbon for each child. Cut one 4-inch (10-cm) length of metallic thread for each child.

Procedures: Assist children in following these instructions: Fold 1 inch (2.5 cm) of longer piece of ribbon back and crease it. Tie ends of metallic thread together. Place tied metallic thread inside the fold and glue folded portion to back of ribbon to form hanger (see sketch a). Fold shorter piece of ribbon in half to find midpoint. Glue center of shorter ribbon across longer ribbon about 5 inches (12.5 cm) from top, forming a cross (see sketch b). Glue clothespin pieces, two pieces wide and flat sides down, onto horizontal bar of ribbon. Repeat procedure on vertical bar of ribbon (see sketch c).

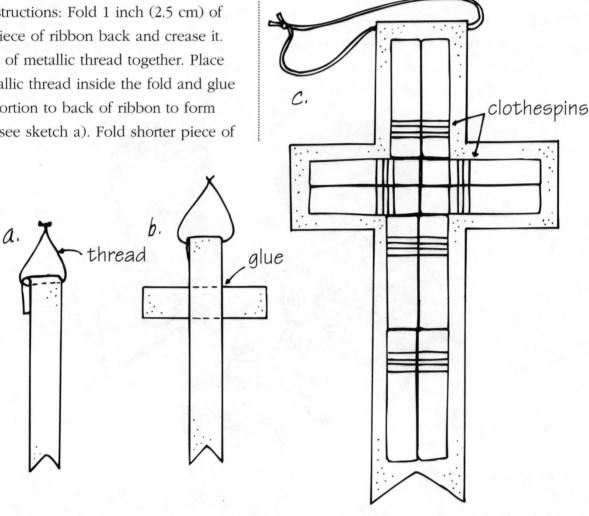

a. thread

b. glue

c. clothespins

Easter Poster

Materials: Bibles, marker, large sheet of paper, construction paper in a variety of colors, pencils and crayons or colored markers, scissors, glue, one large piece of poster board.

Procedure: Brainstorm words, shapes and short sentences that tell about the resurrection of Jesus ("angel," "empty tomb," a flower, a cross, "Jesus is alive!" "Christ is risen!" "Jesus rose so that we can live!"). List children's suggestions on large sheet of paper. (Children may read Mark 15:1-15, 42-47 and 16:1-7 if they need help.)

Ask each child to choose a word, shape or sentence from the list you have made. Children write or draw what they have chosen on a piece of construction paper and then cut around it to make an interesting shape. They glue their shapes to the poster board to make a poster. (Optional: One child writes or makes a title for the poster.) Display the completed poster in a prominent place.

Clothespin Planter

Materials: Newspaper, acrylic paint in several colors, shallow containers, paint smocks or old shirts, one clean 12-ounce tuna can and a small potted plant for each child, glue, wooden clothespins (not spring-type), paintbrushes, potting soil.

Preparation: Cover work area with newspaper. Pour paint into shallow containers.

Procedure: Have children put on paint smocks or old shirts and instruct children to follow these directions: Run a line of glue down the outside of the can and place a clothespin on the glue, fitting it over the edge of the can (see sketch a). Repeat process with clothespins until entire can is covered (see sketch b). After glue has dried, paint clothespins with acrylic paint. Allow the paint to dry thoroughly. Place potted plant and potting soil inside of planter. Discuss with the children why we celebrate Easter. Children decide who they would like to give the planter to as an Easter gift.

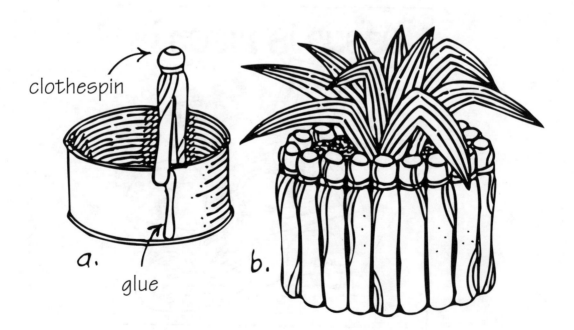

clothespin

a.

glue

b.

Bible Covers

Materials: Scissors, felt, measuring stick, pencils, glue.

Preparation: Cut one 9×13-inch (22.5×32.5-cm) and two 3×9-inch (7.5×22.5-cm) rectangles of felt for each child. (Note: Measurements are for standard-sized Bibles. For other sizes, cut felt pieces 1/2 inch larger than each side of Bibles.)

Procedure: For the cover, have the children choose an Easter story symbol that is simple enough to be cut from felt (heart, cross, fish, dove, etc.). Discuss with children what these symbols mean (heart—love of Jesus, cross—Jesus' crucifixion, fish—Jesus or a believer in Jesus, dove—spirit of God).

Instruct children in the following steps: Draw design on felt scrap and cut out (see sketch a). Squeeze a line of glue on the two short edges and one long edge of both small felt rectangles. Glue each small rectangle to shorter edge of larger rectangle to form pockets of cover (see sketch b). Be sure to leave inside edges unglued. Fold cover in half with pockets on the inside. Glue felt design in place on front of cover (see sketch c). If desired, cut small additional shapes from felt scrap and glue on cover as further decoration. Let glue dry overnight before putting Bible inside the cover.

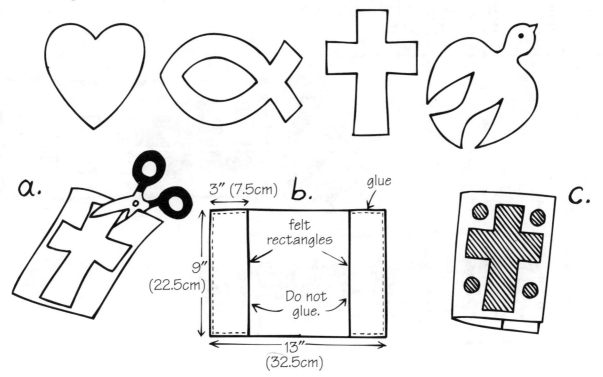

a.

3" (7.5cm)   b.   glue

felt rectangles

9" (22.5cm)

Do not glue.

13" (32.5cm)

c.

Easter Crafts and Activities

Quilled Message

Materials: Paper cutter, colored photocopy paper, ruler, pencils, construction paper, glue.

Preparation: Using a paper cutter, cut photocopy paper into strips approximately 1/4 inch (.625 cm) wide and 8 inches (20 cm) long. Following the directions given below, make the word "Jesus."

Procedure: Show the word "Jesus." Invite children to use the word "Jesus" in a sentence that tells a part of the Easter story. Ask children for short sentences or messages about why Easter is important. Each child chooses a message that he or she wants to share. Children draw their messages in block letters on construction paper (see sketch a). Children coil paper strips around pencils and then glue the paper coils inside the block letters, creating 3-D letters (see sketch b). Children may also choose to coil only the ends of the paper strips and use these to form the letters of the message (see sketch c).

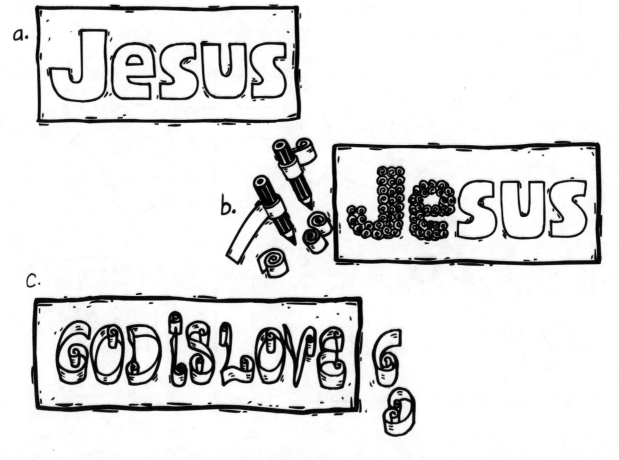

Easter Cards Service Project

Materials: Colored construction paper, markers, Easter stickers, glitter glue, scissors, glue, small individually wrapped candies, envelopes.

Preparation: Arrange with your church pastor for your children to make Easter cards for the shut-ins in your congregation, or speak with the director of a local nursing home or homeless shelter about making the cards for the occupants of that facility.

Procedure: Explain to the children that they will be making cards to share the good news about Jesus with others, and then tell the children who will get the cards they make. Ask children to think of a short message about Easter they can write on their cards. (Jesus is alive! Jesus loves you.) Each child makes one or more Easter cards, printing a short message inside each card and decorating the outside with drawings, stickers and/or glitter glue. Children may also cut simple shapes out of scrap construction paper and glue these to the cards for decoration. Children sign their names inside the cards and place stickers and candies in envelopes with the cards.

Painted Flowerpot

Materials: Newspaper, one 2 1/2-inch (6.25-cm) white plastic flowerpot for each child, paint smocks or old shirts, acrylic paint, paintbrushes, construction paper, markers or crayons, potting soil, small shovel, marigold seeds—two per child, cups, water.

Preparation: Cover work area with newspaper.

Procedure: Give each child a flowerpot. Children put on paint smocks or old shirts. Guide children to paint flowerpots in any design they desire (geometric figures, rainbows, flowers, etc.). While children are working, ask children whom they would like to give their flowerpots to as Easter gifts. While paint is drying, children make cards using construction paper and markers or crayons. Encourage children to suggest sentences to write in the cards to show the joy of Easter. When paint is dry, children fill pots with soil and plant two marigold seeds. Children water seeds and give the pots to the persons of their choice. They may choose to keep pots in a safe place until the marigolds have spouted and then give them away.

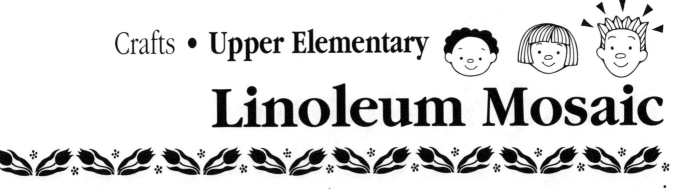

Linoleum Mosaic

Materials: Linoleum scraps, strong scissors or vinyl-cutting tool, paper, pencil, a piece of plywood about 6 inches (15 cm) square for each child, white glue, grout, damp cloths.

Preparation: Cut linoleum scraps into small "tiles."

Procedure: Have children sketch on paper a simple message or design about the Easter story. Children may letter words ("God loves us," for example) and add a decorative border or draw their own designs or symbols. Children then copy the messages or designs onto plywood squares and glue linoleum tiles onto the plywood to fit the design. Some tiles may need to be trimmed as this is done. When the glue has set, children fill the open spaces and cracks with grout and then wipe tiles with a damp cloth.

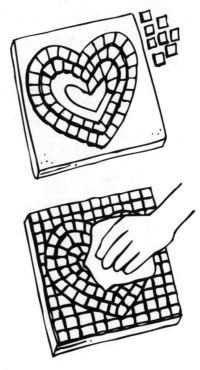

Bread Sculpture

Materials: Waxed paper, one slice of white bread for each child, plastic knives, measuring spoons, white glue, water, paper plates; optional—food coloring, baking sheets, spatula, oven mitt, oven, clear nail polish.

Procedure: Give each child a large sheet of waxed paper to work on and a slice of white bread. Children remove crust with knives and discard. Pour 1 teaspoon of glue and 1/4 teaspoon of water onto each slice of bread. (Optional: Add a few drops of food coloring to dough.) Children knead the bread in their hands until it doesn't stick to their fingers (6 to 10 minutes). As children work, ask them to suggest words that we associate with Easter ("Jesus," "cross," "risen" etc.). Lead children to choose one or more words and assign one or more letters to each child. Children use dough to form their assigned letters. Children place letters on paper plates and arrange paper plates to spell the word(s). Allow letters to dry overnight. (Optional: Place letters on baking sheets and bake at 225° for four minutes.) Children may want to paint dry letters with clear nail polish to preserve them.

Variation: Ask children to suggest shapes that remind them of Easter (cross, heart, etc.). Children complete craft as described above, creating shapes instead of letters.

"I'm a Believer!" Fish

Materials: Raffia (available at craft stores), scissors, measuring stick, index cards, masking tape, craft glue, pens or pencils, hole punch.

Preparation: Cut three 3-foot (.9-m) lengths of raffia for each child. Cut index cards in half lengthwise, one half for each child. Make a sample raffia fish.

Procedure: Show sample raffia fish that you made. **In the days right after Jesus returned to heaven, people were often killed for being Christians. They used a secret symbol to identify other Christians. This symbol was a fish, drawn with two simple arches. When talking with someone, a Christian would draw an arch on the ground with his foot. If the other person drew the other arch with his foot, then both people would know they were talking to another Christian. The Greek word for fish, *ichthus*, was an acrostic for "Jesus Christ, Son of God, Savior."**

Give each child three lengths of raffia. Children tie ends of three lengths of raffia together in a knot, leaving a 1-inch (2.5-cm) tail above knot (see sketch a). Children tape tail of knot onto a hard surface and braid strips loosely until approximately 4 inches (10 cm) are left (see sketch b). After children tie knot at end of braid, they remove tape from braid, hold both ends of braid together to form a fish shape, use craft glue to glue in place and hold until dry (see sketch c). Children then trim ends to leave a small fringe. On index card strips, children write sentence prayers thanking God. Punch holes in each card and attach to fish using additional raffia (see sketch c).

a. 1" (2.5 cm) tie knot

b. tape   (10 cm) 4"

c.
raffia braid in shape of fish

ALLELUIA!

Games

Game Tips

Play and learn! Often children are not aware of the direct learning value of a game, but they participate enthusiastically because they enjoy the game. Games help children discover, use and remember Bible truths and verses; games also help children increase their skills in interacting in a group situation. With the games provided here, your children will have fun and learn at the same time.

- Explain the rules or procedures clearly and simply.

- Offer a practice round, especially if the game is new. Children will learn the rules best by actually playing the game.

- Choose games appropriate to the skill levels of the children involved. If you know that some children are not able to read or write as well as others, avoid playing games which depend solely on that skill for success. When playing a game in which children must answer questions, suggest that the child whose turn it is may answer the question or ask a member of his or her team to answer the question.

- Vary the process by which teams are formed. Allow children to group themselves into teams. Play the game one time; then announce that the person on each team who is wearing the most (blue) should rotate to another team. Play the game again. Vary the method of rotation so that children play with several different children each time.

(These tips are adapted from Gospel Light's reproducible *Sunday School Smart Pages*.)

Discover the Reason

Materials: Bible, small pieces of paper, felt pen, plastic eggs, small pieces of wood, nails, pieces of gauze, stones, Easter stickers.

Preparation: Letter the words of Romans 5:8 on small pieces of paper, several words on each paper. Put one paper you prepared or one object (wood, nail, gauze or stone) into each egg. Place stickers on the eggs containing the words of Romans 5:8. Prepare the same number of eggs as you have children in your group. Hide the eggs in the room or, if possible, in an area outdoors.

Procedure: Children hunt for eggs. Gather children together and open all eggs (reserve eggs with stickers for last). **What part of the Easter story does a piece of wood remind you of?** (The cross on which Jesus was crucified.) **A nail?** (Nails were used to crucify Jesus to the cross.) **This gauze?** (Jesus' body was wrapped in fabric like gauze.) **A stone?** (The entrance to Jesus' tomb was covered by a large rock, but it was rolled away when Jesus rose from the dead.) Children with papers in their eggs put the words of the verse in correct order and then read it aloud. **The words of Romans 5:8 and these objects remind us of the reason we celebrate Easter: Jesus died on the cross and came back to life so that our sins can be forgiven.**

An Eggs-tra Puzzling Hunt!

Materials: Instant camera and film, scissors, envelopes, plastic eggs, Easter stickers.

Preparation: Take photos of different spots around the room or building you are in or of a nearby outdoor area. Take one photo for each child in your group. Cut each photo into puzzle pieces. Put each photo-puzzle in a separate envelope. Put a few stickers inside each egg and hide the eggs in locations illustrated in photos.

Procedure: Give each child one photo-puzzle envelope. At your signal, children put puzzles together and then retrieve their eggs.

The Gift of Easter

Materials: Bibles, small box, wrapping paper, scissors, tape, ribbon.

Preparation: Tape box closed. Cover box with wrapping paper and decorate with ribbon.

Procedure: Show children box you prepared. Let children tell about the best gifts they have received. Explain that we don't often think of Easter as a time for gifts, but that the most special gift we could ever receive was bought for us a long time ago at this time of the year. Help children find Romans 6:23 in their Bibles and read the verse aloud together. Explain that you're going to play a game to help us remember God's Easter gift to us.

Children sit in a semicircle. Ask for a volunteer to be the guesser. The guesser stands in front of the semicircle with his or her back toward the group. Give the wrapped box to one of the children sitting at the end of the semicircle. Children pass the box down the row. At your signal, the children stop passing the box. The child with the box holds it behind him- or herself. To confuse the guesser, all of the children put their hands behind their backs.

The guesser turns around and guesses which child is holding the box (see sketch). To guess, the guesser must say the name of the child in the following adaptation of Romans 6:23: "The gift of God to (name of child in semicircle)." If the guess is correct, the seated group finishes with "is eternal life in Christ Jesus our Lord" and the guesser trades places with the child who had the box. If the guess is incorrect, the seated group remains silent. After three incorrect guesses, the child with the box trades places with the guesser. Repeat game until each child has had a turn being the guesser or as time allows.

Follow That Friend!

Materials: Bible, measuring stick, butcher paper, scissors, marker, tape, small slips of paper, paper bag.

Preparation: Cut a 4-foot (1.2-m) length of butcher paper. Draw a 16-square grid on the butcher paper and letter the words "You," "Friend," "Do" and "Command" in the boxes (see sketch). Make one grid for each group of four children. Tape grid(s) to floor. Also letter the same four words on separate slips of paper. Put paper slips into the paper bag.

Procedure: Discuss ways we show we are friends with others (play with them, help them, treat them kindly, etc.). Explain that right before He died, Jesus told His disciples how they could show they were His friends. Have a volunteer read John 15:14 ("You are my friends if you do what I command."). Repeat the verse with the class several times.

Have children form groups of four. Each group stands around a grid you prepared, one child on each side of the paper (see sketch). The caller (you or a child acting as the caller) chooses a slip of paper from the paper bag and reads the word aloud. The first player around each grid says John 15:14 and then puts his or her hand or foot on a square with that word. The caller puts the slip back into the bag and repeats the process for each additional player. Play continues until all players have all hands and feet on a square or until someone falls over.

Verse Circles

Materials: Bibles, marker, index cards, cassette/CD of children's Christian music, cassette/CD player.

Preparation: Number two identical sets of index cards, making one card for each child in the group.

Procedure: Help children find Romans 5:8 in their Bibles and with the children read the verse aloud. Then read aloud again, asking each child to substitute his or her name (one at a time) in place of the words "we" and "us."

Children form two equal groups. (You may need to join one group.) Groups stand in two concentric circles (see sketch). Give a numbered index card to each child in the inner circle, mixing up the order in which the cards are given. Children keep their numbers secret. Then give the second set of numbers to the children in the outer circle. While music plays, the children in the inner circle walk clockwise and children in outer circle walk counterclockwise. When the music stops, each child must find the child with the matching number. Then pairs repeat the words of Romans 5:8 together. Repeat game several times, assigning new numbers each time. (Optional: After playing the game several times, when pairs find each other they do a verbal verse bounce instead of repeating the verse together: one child says the first word of Romans 5:8 and the other says the next, continuing until they reach the end of the verse.)

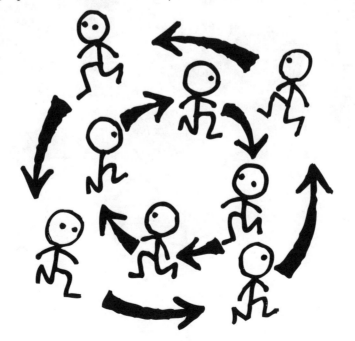

Glad Tag

Materials: None.

Procedure: Teach children the following Easter rhyme: "Don't fear! Be glad! He is not dead!/The Lord is risen as He said!" Repeat with them several times in unison; then have volunteer fill in missing words as you say the rhyme.

Children sit in a circle on the floor. Choose one child to be "It." "It" walks around the outside of the circle while the class repeats the words of the rhyme. Then the child repeats the rhyme as he or she walks around the circle a second time. At any time while repeating the rhyme for the second time, "It" may touch the head of one of the seated children (see sketch). Child who was touched chases "It" around circle one time, trying to tag "It." Whether or not "It" is tagged, he or she sits down in the circle. The child who was touched becomes the new "It." Repeat game until each child has had a turn to be "It." Vary the game by asking each new "It" to tell something about Easter that makes him or her glad.

Guess Who

Materials: Bibles.

Procedure: Have children stand in a circle around you and follow your motions. Begin clapping and then start a new motion every 10 seconds or so, until you have led children through several motions (snapping fingers, nodding head, tapping shoulders, etc.). Then repeat, as children try to follow your motions without looking directly at you all the time. Suggest children look to your side or slowly look around the circle.

By following the leader, you know when to start a new motion in this game. By following Jesus, you know what's right to do and what right choices to make. Just before Jesus was killed on the cross, He told what people who love Him should do. Help children find John 12:26 in

their Bibles and, with children, read the first phrase aloud. **We're going to play a guessing game to help us remember Jesus' words in John 12:26.**

One child stands in the center of the circle and closes his or her eyes. Choose one child to be the leader who begins a motion. Children follow the leader's motions, trying not to make it obvious who the leader is. Leader changes motion every 10 seconds or so. Tell child in center to open his or her eyes and guess who the leader might be. If the guess is incorrect, the guessed child shakes his or her head no. If the guess is correct, the leader responds by repeating the words of John 12:26. After two or three incorrect guesses, choose a new child to be in the center and a new leader.

Go Fish!

Materials: Bibles, Go Fish! Cards Pattern, photocopier, paper, scissors, measuring stick, yarn or string, spring-type clothespin, blanket.

Preparation: Photocopy one Go Fish! Cards Pattern for each child and one for yourself. Cut apart your set of cards. Cut one 3-foot (.9-m) length of yarn or string. Tie one end of the yarn or string to the measuring stick and the other end to the clothespin.

Procedure: Show one of your fish cards and ask a volunteer to describe the situation pictured on the card. **What would you do if this happened to you? Who can we ask to help us make right choices?** (God, parent, teacher, friend, etc.) **Before Jesus was put to death on the cross, he told people how to make good choices.** Help children find John 12:26 in their Bibles. Read verse aloud together. **What might Jesus want you to do in this situation?** Let volunteers answer.

When we try to make right choices, we show we want to obey Jesus.

Distribute scissors and patterns for Go Fish! cards. Children cut apart fish cards. Collect the cards and place them in a pile on the floor. Two children hold a blanket in front of cards and one child (or you) sits by the cards. Give the fishing pole to one of the remaining children. Child casts the clothespin hook over the blanket (see sketch).

The person sitting behind the blanket attaches a fish card to the clothespin and tugs on the string. The fisher pulls in the fish and then tells how he or she could follow Jesus in the pictured situation. If a child catches the fish card with the star on it, he or she gets an extra turn to fish or repeats John 12:26.

71

Hidden Messages

Materials: Large sheet of paper, felt pen, 8 1/2×11-inch (21.5×27.5-cm) paper, pencils.

Preparation: Letter large sheet of paper as shown in sketch.

Procedure: Show children the large sheet of paper you prepared and ask them what is wrong with the sentence. Have volunteers take turns crossing out every other letter. Another volunteer reads aloud the hidden sentence ("GOOD NEWS—JESUS IS ALIVE!"). Discuss the different ways we celebrate Jesus' resurrection. Give each child a piece of paper and a pencil. Instruct children to think of a sentence telling something about Easter, Jesus' death and resurrection or God's love for all people. Then they write the sentence with extra letters to make other hidden messages. Help children as needed to complete the assignment. Then have children trade papers with each other to discover the sentences. Read children's hidden sentences aloud.

BGAOPOHD XNTEVWBS-

LJOEGSBUPS OINS

TASLGINVDE!

Sentence, Anyone?

Materials: Bibles, felt pens, small index cards, chalk and chalkboard or marker and paper, box or other container.

Preparation: Write each word of this sentence on a separate index card: "Jesus is risen from the dead."

Procedure: Mix up the cards you made and ask volunteers to tell you what the correct sentence order of the words should be. Read the completed sentence aloud. Instruct children to think of other sentences that are about the Easter story and that are six or fewer words long. Write children's suggestions on chalkboard or paper. Read and ask questions about verses from Mark 16:1-8 and John 20:1-18 if children need help thinking of sentences. Brainstorm sentences with children until at least one sentence has been suggested for each pair of children in the group.

Then assign one or two sentences to each pair of children. Distribute felt pens and index cards. Children write each word of their assigned sentences on separate index cards.

Collect all the cards, mix them together and place them facedown in a box or other container. Each pair of players takes six cards from the box and tries to make a sentence (all cards need not be used). If players cannot make a sentence, they choose a new card and discard one they do not want. Each pair receives one point for each card used in a sentence. Game ends when all players have made a sentence. If time permits, play game again.

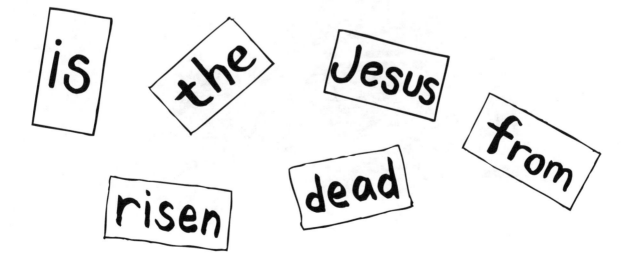

Host a Hunt

Materials: Small slips of paper, markers, plastic eggs, Easter stickers, individually wrapped candies or other small treats.

Preparation: Arrange for your children to host an Easter egg hunt for younger children. Find out how many children are in the group your children will be hosting and make sure that there are at least the same number of eggs as there are children (plan for visitors also).

Procedure: Children brainstorm and then write simple messages about Jesus on slips of paper. ("Jesus loves you!" "Jesus is alive!") Children fill each plastic egg with a slip of paper, a few stickers and one or two candies or other treats. Then children hide Easter eggs in a room or outdoor area and invite the younger children to find them. Before the hunt begins, tell the younger children the number of eggs that they may find and keep. Once all the eggs have been collected, have the older children help the younger ones read the sentences they have found in their eggs.

Answer Match

Materials: Large sheet of paper, marker, large Post-it Notes, pencils, a coin or small beanbag.

Preparation: Letter the following questions on a large sheet of paper: "What's one Easter tradition your family likes to celebrate?" "What's your favorite part of the Easter story?" "What's one reason you are glad that Jesus is alive?" "What is one important thing people need to know about Jesus?"

Procedure: Give each child several Post-it Notes. Each child writes an answer to each question on a separate Post-it Note.

After children have written answers, collect Post-it Notes and arrange them on the floor in a grid. Children take turns tossing a coin or small beanbag onto the grid and guessing which question is answered on the note the coin lands on.

After children have matched answers to questions, invite children to choose one of the notes to take home as a prayer reminder.

Matching Dots

Materials: Bibles, self-stick dots (or Post-it Notes) in several colors, chairs, index cards, marker.

Preparation: Place chairs in a circle. Randomly distribute an equal number of colors of dots, one on each chair. Letter the following questions on index cards: "What's one Easter tradition your family likes to celebrate?" "What's your favorite part of the Easter story?" "What's one reason you are glad that Jesus is alive?" "What is one important thing people need to know about Jesus?" "What is your favorite song about Easter?" Place a different-colored dot on each index card.

Procedure: Children sit on chairs with colored dots. Choose an index card. Child sitting on the chair with dot of that color reads the question to the group. Then the child (or a volunteer sitting in a chair having a dot of the same color) answers the question. Continue choosing cards and having different children read and answer questions.

ALLELUIA!

Activities

Activity Tips

The activities on these pages offer a variety of ways to help children understand the real reason for celebrating Easter—Jesus is alive! Through the hands-on experiences of drama, art, music and writing, children achieve a clearer understanding of biblical truth and are able to better relate it to their own lives.

• Acting allows children to make Bible stories and truths come alive; and by having a "firsthand" experience, children will better remember the story or truth—and better understand it. Role-playing situations also help children to concretely express abstract concepts like love, friendliness and sharing.

• Drawing and painting allow children to express thoughts or feelings that may be difficult to put into words and help them visualize specific actions to apply to Bible truths.

• Singing songs helps children memorize Scripture, learn Bible truths and enjoy times of prayerful inspiration and quiet thanksgiving.

• Writing can help children organize what they are learning as well as give them an opportunity to express what they think and feel about God or about their own experiences and needs.

Use these activities as springboards to bring the glorious truth of Easter home to your children.

• Know the learning purpose of each activity. Be able to explain *why* you are doing the activity, not just *what* you are doing.

• Guide the conversation during the activity to accomplish that purpose. Encourage children to talk about what they are doing and thinking, and listen attentively to what they say.

• Near the end of the activity, have children put into their own words what they have learned.

Bean Sprouts

Materials: Bible, paper towels, shallow containers, water, quart-size resealable plastic bags, lima beans, masking tape, marker.

Preparation: For each child, fold a paper towel in half two times. Fill shallow containers with water.

Procedure: Children sprinkle water on folded paper towels until they are damp. Children dry hands, place dampened towels in plastic bags and then put five beans in bag as shown in sketch. Beans should not touch each other. Seal each child's bag. On each bag, put a masking tape strip with child's name and instructions to add water every two to four days. Child takes bag home. Talk about things for which we can praise the Lord.

What's helping you to make your towel wet? Yes! God made your hands to help you and He made the water. And we can praise the Lord for our hands and for everything He made. Open your Bible. **Our Bible tells us that it is good to praise the Lord. On the first Palm Sunday, people shouted praises to Jesus as He rode into Jerusalem.**

Flower Surprises

Materials: Supplies for the planting activity you choose.

Preparation: Choose one of the planting activities described below and gather all necessary supplies. If necessary, make arrangements to use an area of the church property for the activity.

Procedure: Do you know what is one of the prettiest things we see in the spring? Flowers start to grow and bloom! Who created all the plants and flowers we see? That's right—God did! And we can thank God for all the pretty plants and flowers in the world! We're going to plant some (seeds), so we can watch them grow and bloom. Help children as necessary to complete the activity you chose.

1. Plant flower seeds in potting soil in cardboard egg cartons (see sketch a). Keep the soil moist. When seedlings appear, cut egg cartons apart and plant in the ground. The cardboard will dissolve. (Optional: Cut egg cartons apart after seedlings appear and have each child take one section home to plant in his or her yard.)

2. Explain to children that bulbs are like big seeds. Plant bulbs in a large planter in your room (see sketch b) or in a section of the church property. Work together to care for the flowers as they grow.

3. Plant seeds in worked soil on the church property (see sketch c), following the instructions on the seed packet(s). Have children help weed the area and water the plants as they grow.

a.

b.

c.

Scent Sense

Materials: Cotton balls, small containers (empty plastic pill bottles or film canisters) or resealable plastic bags, food flavoring extracts (maple, orange, lemon, vanilla, cherry, spearmint, etc.), vinegar, perfume, box.

Preparation: Saturate each cotton ball with a different scent. Place one cotton ball in each container or bag. Place containers or bags in box.

Procedure: Child smells and identifies scents. **What food does this smell remind you of? Who made your nose? God did! God made your nose so that you can smell things. Does this smell like flowers to you? God made flowers for us. We thank God for making flowers. But we thank God most of all that Jesus is living. We are happy at Eastertime because Jesus has risen.**

Going Shopping

Materials: Old purses and wallets, grocery bags and/or empty boxes and bags from stores in a local mall.

Procedure: Children act out going to the grocery store or to a mall, buying foods and/or gifts for Easter.

I like to go shopping. Do you like to go shopping? It's fun to go shopping for Easter treats for our families and friends. What do you like to buy at Eastertime? I like to buy Easter lilies. I like to buy things to make Easter treats, too. Easter is such a special time. Easter is when we remember that Jesus died and lives again.

Rhythm Instruments

Materials: Cassette/CD of Easter music, cassette/CD player, rhythm instruments (small drums, drumsticks, musical triangles, tambourines, maracas); optional—small boxes, unsharpened pencils or wooden spoons, metal hangers, wire whisks, sturdy paper plates, yarn, scissors, bells, baby rattles or plastic film canisters, beads and tape.

Preparation: None. (Optional: If instruments are not available, substitutions can be used. Instead of drums, children can use small boxes. Unsharpened pencils or wooden spoons can be tapped together instead of drumsticks. In place of musical triangles, tap metal hangers with wire whisks. Tambourines can be made by attaching a few bells to sturdy paper plates. Baby rattles or plastic film canisters partly filled with beads and securely taped can substitute for maracas.)

Procedure: Play Easter music. Demonstrate how to use rhythm instruments. **There are so many happy Easter songs. We like Easter music because it tells about how Jesus died and lives again.** Give children instruments to play and encourage the children to play the instruments in time with the music. When children are comfortable playing the instruments, guide them in walking around in a parade while playing the instruments. **I love to play music about how Jesus died and lives again. God loved us and sent Jesus to be our Savior. Easter is such a happy time!**

Blocks Road

Materials: Fabric, measuring stick, scissors, blocks; optional—large solid-colored T-shirts.

Preparation: Make a Bible-times costume for each child by folding in half a 2×4-foot (.6×1.2-m) piece of fabric and cutting a hole in the center of the fold (see sketch a). (Optional: Use large solid-colored T-shirts for costumes.) Tie a long strip of fabric as a sash or belt around each child's waist (see sketch b).

Procedure: Children use blocks to outline a road (see sketch c). Tell the Bible story about the first Palm Sunday and guide children to act it out. Children wear Bible-times costumes.

The children on the first Palm Sunday were happy to walk down the road with Jesus. Let's make a special road like the one Jesus rode His donkey on. Let's pretend we're putting palm branches on the road. That's what the people in our Bible did. Our Bible says to sing praises to the Lord. People were happy to see Jesus. They said a special word, "hosanna." This is another way to praise Jesus. Let's say that word together.

a.

cut

b.

c.

Mirror Talk

Materials: Bible, several large hand-held unbreakable mirrors.

Procedure: Lead children in repeating, "Mirror, mirror, who do you see? I see a happy face looking at me." Demonstrate this activity by making faces as you look in the mirror. Each child looks in a mirror and makes a happy face. Repeat rhyme several times, each time calling out a description of a different kind of face (surprised, angry, sad, scared, etc.).

Our Bible tells us about a time when some angry people hurt Jesus. How do you think Jesus' friends felt when they heard that Jesus had been hurt so badly that He died? Hold up mirror. Say rhyme, using the feelings children discussed. Hold open Bible. **Later our Bible says, "Jesus is risen again." That means that after Jesus died, He lived again! How do you think Jesus' friends felt when He came back to life?** Repeat rhyme with the description of a surprised face and then a happy face.

After making the happy face, say, **I am glad because I know that Jesus is alive. Let's tell God thank-you that Jesus is alive. Dear God, thank You for making Jesus alive. In Jesus' name, amen.** Encourage children to repeat this short prayer after you.

Welcome the King

Materials: Bible, watering can, water, any variety of potted palm tree or plant (or branches cut from a palm tree), magnifying glass; optional—pictures of palm trees from encyclopedias or Bible-times books, plate, pitted dates.

Preparation: Fill watering can half full of water.

Procedure: Have children gather around the tree or plant (or branches). **Have you ever seen a palm tree? How does the branch feel? Let's look at a branch through the magnifying glass.** Children touch palm tree or plant and take turns examining branches, using magnifying glass. Children take turns watering palm. (Optional: Show pictures of large palm trees.) **In the country where Jesus lived, there are many palm trees.** (Optional: Explain that some palm trees grow fruits called dates on them. Arrange dates on a plate for children to sample. While children eat, look at pictures of palm trees and talk about the first Palm Sunday.)

In Bible times when people welcomed a king, they cut palm branches and put them on the road for the king to walk on. Hold open Bible. **The Bible tells about a time when people put palm branches on the ground when Jesus was coming to town. Let's pretend to put palm branches down for Jesus to walk on. Children pretend to lay branches on the floor and welcome Jesus to town.**

Build a Town

Materials: Bible, blocks, plastic or wooden people figures and cars.

Procedure: Children build a pretend town. Suggest they build places children go (home, church, library, grocery store, mall, etc.). Help children name places where Jesus is with them.

Hold open Bible. **Our Bible tells us that Jesus died and lives again. Just before He went back to heaven, Jesus said, "I am with you always." Our town has many places to go. Where is your favorite place to go? The (library) is a fun place. Is Jesus with you when you go to (the library), (Alison)? Yes, Jesus is always with us. Is Jesus with you, (Timmy), when you go to (the grocery store)? Yes, Jesus is always with us.** Continue naming places and children until everyone has been included.

Real or Unreal?

Materials: Bible, sets of real and artificial items (a real flower/an artificial flower, a real [hard-boiled] egg/a plastic egg, plastic play food/pretzels or crackers, etc.).

Preparation: Place items on a low table so that children can examine them.

Procedure: Children examine items and decide which items are real and which are not real. Talk about things that are real, or true.

Which of these flowers do you think is real? Why? God gave us eyes and fingers and noses to see and feel and smell to know if a flower is real. **Is this flower a real flower?** Point to other items. Invite children to tell how they know each item is or is not real. **One day one of Jesus' friends used her eyes to SEE that Jesus was alive. She used her ears to hear Jesus talk. She found out that it was real: Jesus was alive again after He had died.** Open your Bible. **Our Bible says it this way: "It is true! The Lord has risen."**

Walk the Path

Materials: Masking tape.

Preparation: Make a path by laying masking tape on floor in parallel lines about 10 to 12 inches (20 to 25 cm) apart. Extend path and add curves and turns as long as space permits.

Procedure: Lead children in walking down the path without stepping on the tape. Then invite children to follow other actions you demonstrate, such as hopping, tiptoeing, walking backwards, etc. If a child steps out of the lines simply comment, "It's hard to stay in the lines."

Use the path to briefly tell about Jesus' death, focusing on the Resurrection portion of the story. **Jesus' friends were very sad. Can you walk along the path slowly and sadly? They didn't know Jesus was going to be alive again very soon! But three days later, Mary walked to the place where Jesus' body had been placed. It was called a tomb. Mary looked in. There was NO ONE there! She hurried to tell Jesus' friends, "The tomb is empty!" Some of them ran to the tomb. Let's run down the path like Jesus' friends.**

Continue leading children in this activity as long as time permits.

Follow Me

Materials: Bible, masking tape.

Preparation: Make two parallel masking tape lines on the floor 6 to 8 feet (1.8 to 2.4 m) apart.

Procedure: Children move from one line to the other in a variety of ways. Suggest children tiptoe, crawl, slide, walk backwards, jump, etc. While children are moving, talk with them about ways Jesus shows He loves them. Give each child a chance to make up a movement for the others to copy. The child who is the leader says "Follow me." Other children follow the leader, copying his or her movements. Then a new leader is chosen and makes up a different movement for children to copy. If a child cannot think of a different movement, help him or her to select one that has been used already.

Let's see if we can (jump) from this line to that one. You're good at (jumping). I like to wiggle and move! It makes me glad! Hold open Bible. **In our Bible we can read about what made a man named Thomas glad. Jesus came to see Thomas so that Thomas could see for himself that Jesus wasn't dead any more, that He is alive. Our Bible tells us that when Thomas saw Jesus he said, "My Lord and my God!" Thomas was glad Jesus was alive again. And Thomas was glad that Jesus loved him. I'm glad Jesus loves me, too.**

Jesus Lives

The Bible says that Jesus died

For me and you and you.

POINT TO SEVERAL OTHERS.

The Bible says He is alive!

It's true! It's true! It's true!

CLAP ON "TRUE."

The Bible says that Jesus lives.

He sees us while we play;

He cares for us when we're asleep;

He listens when we pray!

The Bible says that Jesus loves

Us all—yes, me and you.

And someday He will come again!

It's true! It's true! It's true! CLAP ON "TRUE."

Spring

The bunnies hop and nibble grass.

Chicks peck to hatch from eggs.

TAP INSIDE OF CUPPED HAND.

The sun shines warm; the puppies run;

The kittens yawn and stretch their legs.

In spring, we might put on new clothes.

To grandma's house we drive.

But best of all, we hear good news:

"Jesus is alive!"

Easter

We tiptoe quietly to the tomb.

We are so very sad.

But look! There is an angel

Who's telling us, "Be glad!

Jesus isn't here now.

He is alive, not dead!"

We run to tell the others!

"He's risen, as He said!"

Jesus Is Living

Joyfully today we sing,

Jesus is our risen King!

Jesus is living!

Yes, He is living!

Jesus is living!

We praise Him today!

INSTANT SONG: Sing to the tune of "Jesus Loves Me," repeating first two lines for the stanza.

Jesus Gives

Jesus gives me food each day

And many places I can play

And a home where I can live

And people who have love to give.

He gives me stars that shine above.

Thank you, Jesus, for Your love.

Jesus Loves Us All

Who are the people Jesus loves?

Jesus loves us all!

He loves us if we're very short;

He loves us if we're tall.

He loves folks with curly hair

And those whose hair is straight.

He loves babies who only crawl;

He loves kids who can roller-skate.

He loves us when we're all grown up

And when we don't feel well.

Yes, Jesus loves us all the time—

That's what the Bible tells.

The Happy Parade

Here is the donkey  MAKE CLOPPING SOUNDS.

Clip-clopping along.

The children are skipping

And singing a song.

Here are the branches;

Oh, see how they sway!

Here rides the Lord Jesus

On this happy day.

Day and Night

When the sun is in the sky,

Jesus loves me. HUG SELF.

When the stars are way up high,

Jesus loves me. HUG SELF.

In the day and in the night,

While I play and then sleep tight,

Jesus loves me. HUG SELF. "RUN" FINGERS.

Jesus Is with Me

Jesus is with me

When I sleep.

Jesus is with me

When I play. "RUN" HANDS.

Jesus is with me

All the time,

Every night and

Every day!

Child colors puppets, cuts puppets apart on lines, folds each puppet on fold line and then glues craft stick inside each one. Child builds tomb with blocks and then uses puppets to play out the action of the Easter story.

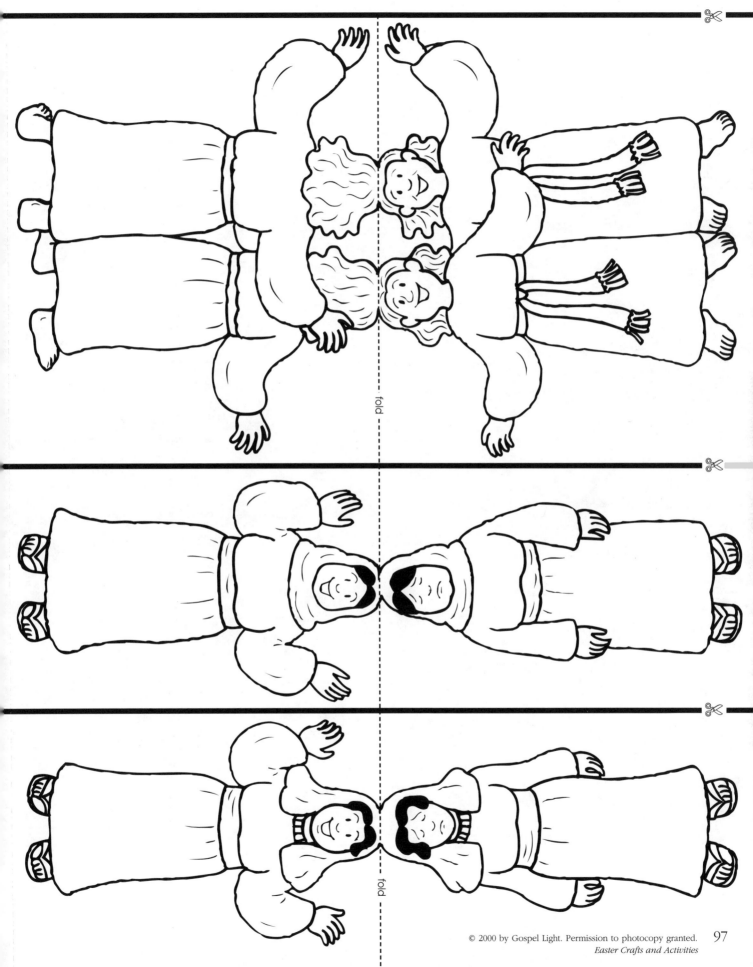

fold

fold

97

Easter Crafts and Activities

Dot glue
here.
Place stick
here.

Dot glue
here.

Dot glue
here.
Place stick
here.

Dot glue
here.

Dot glue
here.
Place stick
here.

Dot glue
here.

Jesus is with me...

Jesus is with me...

Jesus is with me...

Draw a picture of another place Jesus is with you.

99

Child colors page and draws a picture in the blank space.

Name _____

"Jesus said, 'I am with you always.'" (See Matthew 28:20.)

cut

cut

cut

Child colors wall of building scene and three small scenes on bottom of strip. Assist child to cut strip from bottom and cut slits at window sides. Assist child in placing strip in slits to see scenes. (Optional: Child draws him- or herself in blank window space.) **Our Bible tells us, "Jesus said, 'I am with you always.'" Is Jesus with us while we sleep? while we play? while we read?**

Name _____

"Worship the Lord." Luke 4:8

When _____ worships the Lord.
        (Name)

_____ thanks God,
   (Name)

Child colors page, adding hair to the child and drawing in the thought balloon two or three things for which the child is thankful. Assist child as needed to letter his or her name on blank lines.

What are some other ways to worship the Lord?

Draw a picture of something that makes you want to thank God.

Name _____

Child draws and colors picture of item(s) for which he or she can thank God. Child colors rest of page. **Can you sing a song of praise to God about the thing(s) you're thankful for?**

C   G⁷   C

God   is   so   good.   God   is   so   good.

F   C   G⁷   C

God   is   so   good.*   He's   so   good   to   me.

*Substitute one of these phrases (or similar ones) for third phrase: "God has made me" or "God made my hands."

Child colors both sides of page
and then cuts page to make
sequencing puzzle.

"I will sing of

the Lord's great | love forever." Psalm 89:1

Easter Crafts and Activities

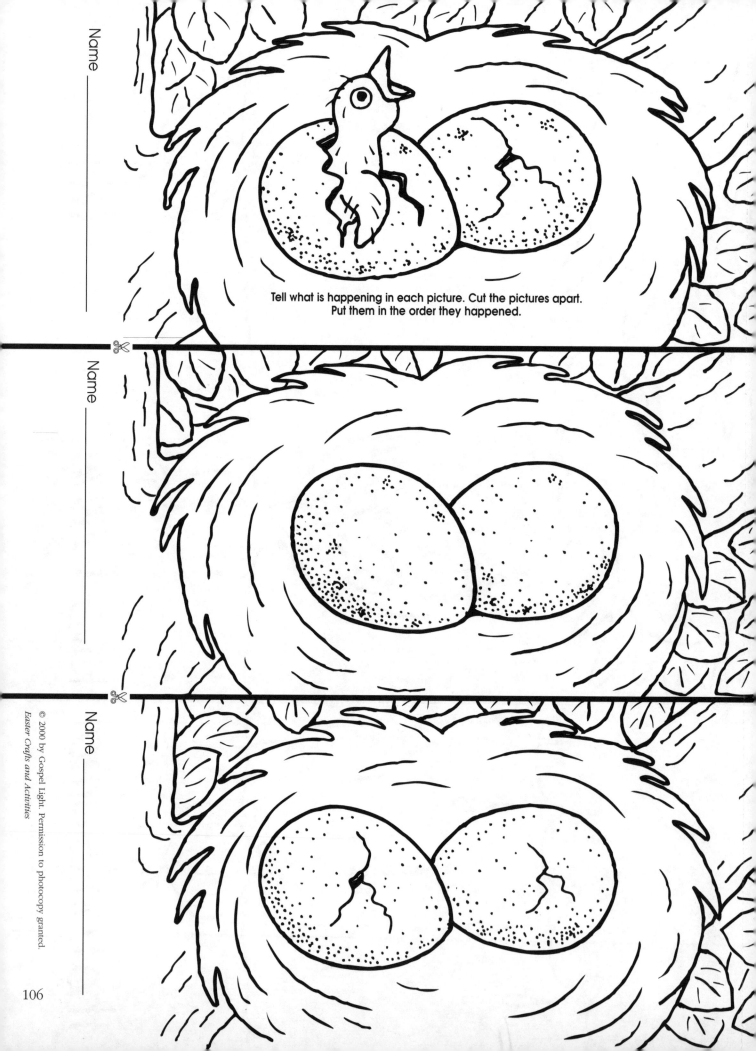

Tell what is happening in each picture. Cut the pictures apart.
Put them in the order they happened.

© 2000 by Gospel Light. Permission to photocopy granted.
Easter Crafts and Activities

Scene 2

"Jesus is risen from the dead."

(See Matthew 28:7.)

Child colors pictures. Child folds on lines. (Optional: Child adds fabric scraps to women's garments.)

Child folds page so that Scene 1 shows on front. Point to sad women. **Why do you think these women are sad? Where are they going? Open the fold. Who do you see?** (Angels.)

Child folds over here. →

Name _____

- fold -

Scene 1

Scene 1

Scene 2

"Thomas said to Jesus, 'My Lord and my God!'"

(See John 20:28.)

Tape top of Jesus figure here.

Tape Thomas figure on this line.

Scene 1:
How do you think Jesus' friends felt when they knew Jesus was alive?

Scene 2:
What did Jesus' friends tell Thomas? What did Thomas say?

Scene 3:
What did Thomas say to Jesus?

Child colors figures and scene, cuts off figures and then tapes figures as shown. Child moves figures to retell Bible story action.

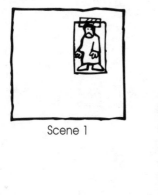

Scene 1

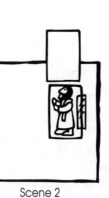

Scene 2

Scene 3

Name _____

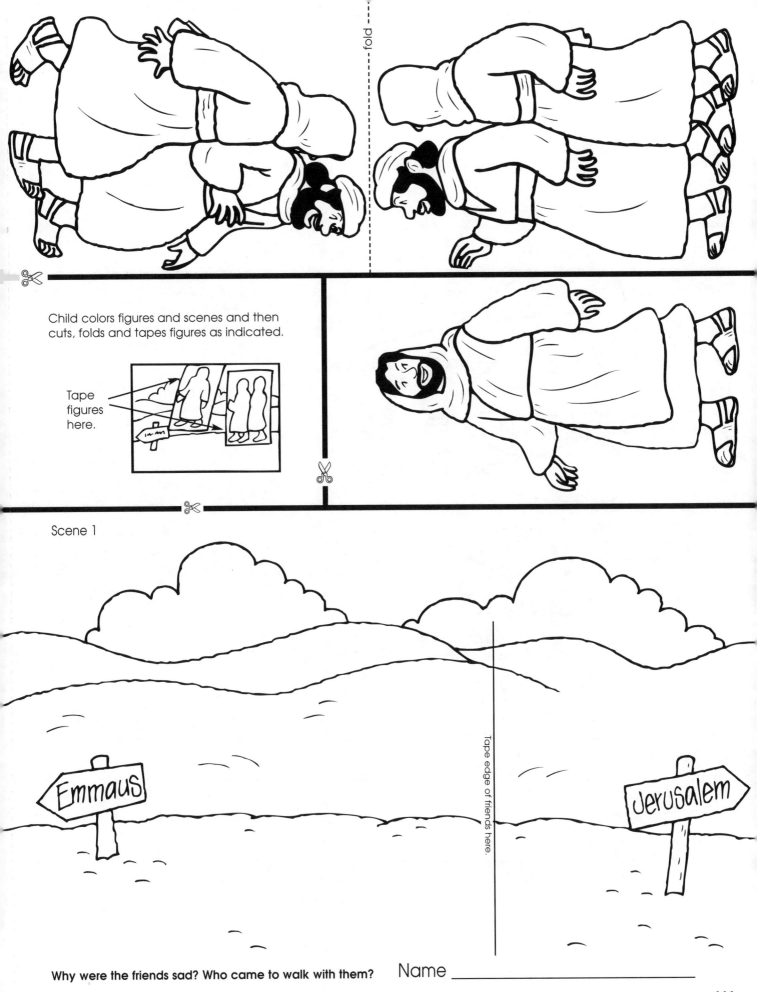

Child colors figures and scenes and then cuts, folds and tapes figures as indicated.

Tape figures here.

Scene 1

Emmaus

Jerusalem

Tape edge of friends here.

Why were the friends sad? Who came to walk with them?

Name _____

Scene 2

Tape here

"Jesus said, 'I am alive for ever and ever!'" (See Revelation 1:18.)

When did the friends know it was Jesus? Then what did they do?

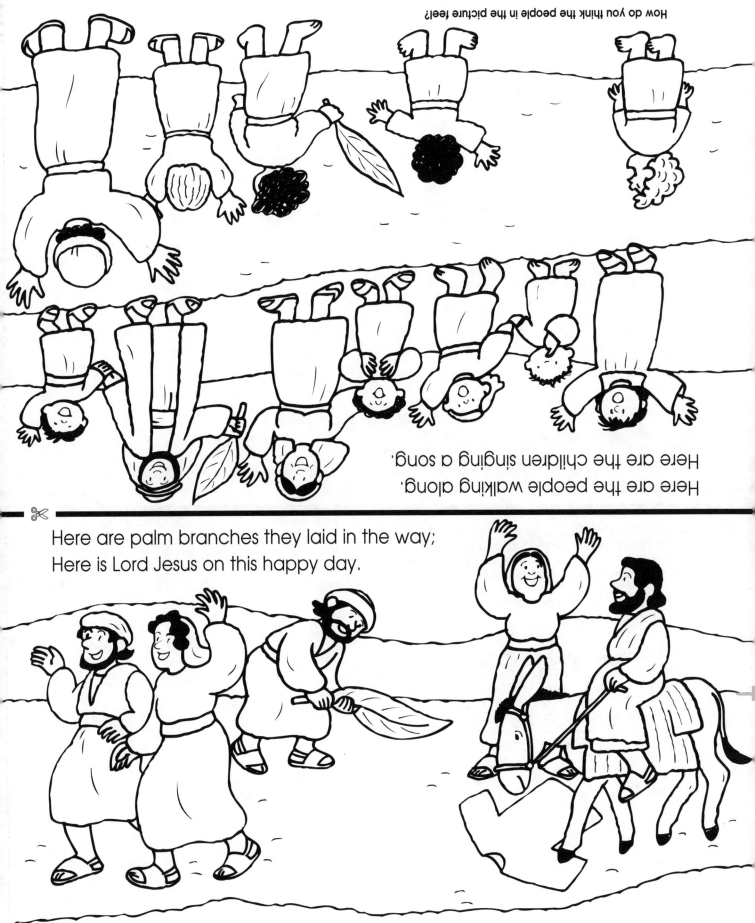

How do you think the people in the picture feel?

Here are the people walking along.
Here are the children singing a song.

Here are palm branches they laid in the way;
Here is Lord Jesus on this happy day.

What word did the people shout to Jesus? (Hosanna.)

"It is good to praise the Lord." Psalm 92:1

fold

Prefold page for child. Child colors scene, adding palm branches and coats to road. Child cuts page on cutting line, matches dot to dot and star to star and tapes the two pieces together. Assist child as needed. (Optional: Child tapes string for donkey's tail and glues fabric to coats.) Refold page to make a stand-up scene.

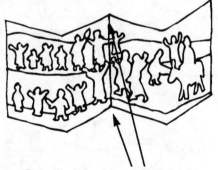

Tape the two pieces together here.

Name _____

Easter Crafts and Activities

"Give thanks to the Lord, for he is good."

Psalm 136:1

Why do you think people put their coats and palm branches on the road?

What happy word did people say?

cut

fold

fold

Name _____

115

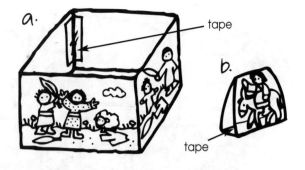

a.

tape

b.

tape

Child colors scenes and then cuts and folds
as indicated. Child tapes pieces together to
make a tabletop theater (see sketch a). Child
colors, cuts out, folds and tapes Jesus figure
(see sketch b). Child plays out story action,
using the tabletop theater and Jesus figure.
(Optional: Child glues cotton to cloud and
sheep.)

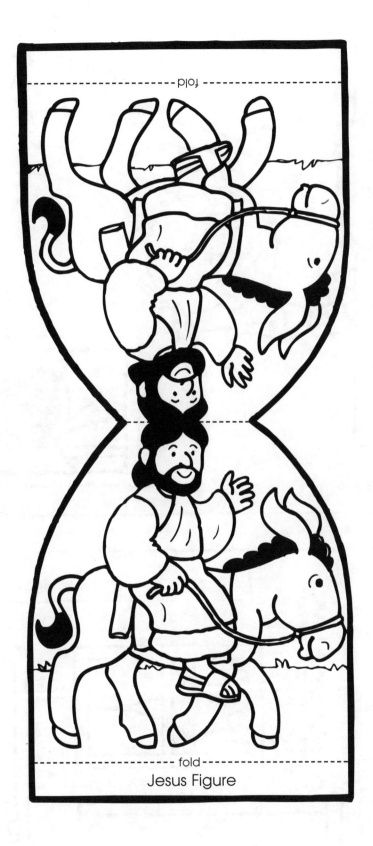

fold

fold

Jesus Figure

"**Jesus is risen from the dead.**" (See Matthew 28:7.)
"**Jesus is living.**" (See Mark 16:6.)

Draw a line around the picture that shows why we celebrate Easter. Color the picture.

Name _____

People welcome Jesus to Jerusalem.
Matthew 21:1-11; Mark 11:1-11; Luke 19:28-44

Jesus dies on the cross.

Matthew 27:32-56; Mark 15:21-41;
Luke 23:26-49; John 19:17-37

Jesus talks to Mary in the garden.

John 20:10-18

Jesus talks to His friends.
Mark 16:14; Luke 24:36-43; John 20:19-23

Thomas believes when he sees Jesus.

John 20:24-29

Jesus goes back to heaven.
Luke 24:50-53; Acts 1:1-11

"I go and prepare a place for you." John 14:3

"Praise the Lord. How good it is to sing praises to our God." Psalm 147:1

"For God so loved the world that he gave his one and only Son, that whoever believes in him shall not perish but have eternal life." John 3:16

"Therefore, if anyone is in Christ, he is a new creation."
2 Corinthians 5:17

Extra! Extra!

Materials: Newspaper, wide-tip markers in a variety of bright colors.

Procedure: Show the newspaper to the children. **What kinds of stories are there in the newspaper?** (Important events, sports, interesting stories about people, etc.) **If you were a reporter, how would you tell the different events that happened in the Easter story?**

Each child pretends to be a newspaper writer and tells what headlines and articles he or she would write about Easter. Write children's answers in big letters on the newspaper. Children draw pictures to go along with their headlines and articles. Talk about why Easter is important.

Praise Parade!

Materials: Bible, marker, index cards, rhythm instruments (small drums, drumsticks, musical triangles, tambourines, maracas); optional—small boxes, unsharpened pencils or wooden spoons, metal hangers, wire whisks, sturdy paper plates, yarn, scissors, bells, baby rattles or plastic film canisters, beads and tape.

Preparation: Letter each word or phrase of Psalm 71:23 onto separate index cards, making one card for each child in your group of up to 12 children. (Optional: If instruments are not available, substitutions can be used. Instead of drums, children can use small boxes. Unsharpened pencils or wooden spoons can be tapped together instead of drumsticks. In place of musical triangles, tap metal hangers with wire whisks. Tambourines can be made by attaching a few bells to sturdy paper plates. Baby rattles or plastic film canisters partly filled with beans and securely taped can substitute for maracas.)

Procedure: Briefly review the story of Palm Sunday, emphasizing the parade of people who were praising Jesus. Have children brainstorm reasons we have to praise Jesus at home, at school, at church, etc. Tell children about a time when you feel like praising or thanking Jesus. Read Psalm 71:23 aloud and have children repeat it with you. Say, **Let's have a Praise Parade!**

Then distribute index cards you prepared and let children put them in order. Collect and shuffle the cards and let each child choose one. Children keep their cards hidden as they stand around the perimeter of the room. Child with the first word or phrase of the verse ("My" or "My lips") is the leader of the parade and places his or her index card faceup on a table or the floor and chooses a rhythm instrument.

Parade leader plays instrument and walks around the room asking children to tell the word(s) on their cards. The child with the next word or phrase places his or her card in order on the table or floor and joins the parade by choosing a rhythm instrument. The leader and the second child walk around the room. The second child asks the remaining children to tell the word(s) on their cards. Repeat process until each child has joined the parade and the verse cards have been placed in order. Parade members say Psalm 71:23 together. As time permits, collect index cards and redistribute them.

Easter Outreach Tree

Materials: Scissors, ruler, yarn, small white tree, tree stand, stickers with Christian Easter pictures and symbols, markers, large sheet of paper, small pieces of light-colored paper, plastic eggs, individually wrapped candies, tape, Easter card, instant camera and film.

Preparation: Cut yarn into 6-inch (15-cm) lengths. Place tree in stand, making sure it is secure. Arrange to deliver the completed tree to a shut-in or person in need of encouragement.

Procedure: Show Easter stickers. Children brainstorm phrases that describe the parts of the Easter story the stickers illustrate. ("Jesus is alive!" "Jesus loves us." "Jesus is our Savior.") Write phrases

on large sheet of paper and place in a visible place. Children choose a phrase and copy it onto a piece of colored paper. Children fill eggs with paper messages, candy and stickers. Help children make hangers with yarn and tape them to the eggs. Children decorate the tree with the eggs. Take a picture of the group decorating the tree.

When tree is finished being decorated, children sign their names to the Easter card. Slip the photo inside the Easter card and then address the card to the shut-in or person in need of encouragement.

Touch and Feel Pictures

Materials: Bible, large sheet of paper, markers, 8×10-inch (20×25-cm) pieces of poster board or card stock, glue, tape, a variety of different-textured materials (fabric scraps, yarn, buttons, lace, rickrack, toothpicks, colored construction paper scraps, cotton, chenille wires, etc.).

Preparation: Review the story of Jesus' resurrection and His appearance to His disciples (John 20:1-28).

Procedure: Listen to the following Bible verses as I read them and get ready to tell what the verses say about Jesus. Read 1 Corinthians 15:3,4. **What did you learn from these verses about Jesus?** Let volunteers answer. **These verses tell us that the most important thing we can know about Jesus is that He died and was raised from the dead. What do you know about that first Easter when Jesus came back to life?** Letter children's responses on large sheet of paper, listing the main events of the story in order.

Each child chooses one of the Easter story events and illustrates it in a touch-and-feel picture by gluing and/or taping a variety of materials onto a piece of poster board or card stock.

When children have completed their touch-and-feel pictures, pictures in story order can be taped together at the edges to make several double or triple stand-up displays (see sketch).

Singing Praise

Materials: Cassette/CD of children's Christian music, cassette/CD player, large sheet of butcher paper, felt pen, scratch paper.

Preparation: Letter the words of a simple song from the cassette/CD on butcher paper, leaving room for two more stanzas on the paper.

Procedure: On the first Palm Sunday, who were the people glad to see? (Jesus.) **How did they show they were glad to see Him?** (Shouted praises. Put coats and branches on the road.) **Why do we want to praise, or say good things about, Jesus?** (He loves us.) **One of the many ways we can praise Jesus is by singing.** Play the song you have chosen from the cassette/CD several times. Invite the children to sing along until they are familiar with the music. **You can write a song of praise to Jesus, too!** Ask children to suggest sentences that tell what happened on the first Palm Sunday. Write children's suggestions on scratch paper. Rewrite sentences as needed and write the new stanza on the butcher paper. Sing the song again, this time singing the new stanza.

Then guide children to write a stanza about reasons children praise Jesus. **What are some things you praise Jesus for? What has Jesus done for you? Why is Jesus special?** Write the new stanza on butcher paper. Sing song using the new stanza. Then sing the entire song.

Jesus is living in heaven today.
How do I know? How do I know?
Jesus is living in heaven today.
The Bible tells me so.

Jesus is always

Praise Puzzles

Materials: Praise Puzzles Pattern (double-sided), photocopier, paper, crayons, scissors.

Preparation: Photocopy one double-sided pattern for each child and one for yourself.

Procedure: Use your copy of the pattern to show children both pictures and briefly discuss the events of Palm Sunday.

Group children in pairs. Give each child a Praise Puzzle Pattern. Children color both sides and then, following the lines on the page, children cut patterns apart to make puzzle pieces. Place all puzzle pieces in a pile on the floor. Pairs sit together on the floor in a circle around the pieces (see sketch).

Have each child in a pair choose to be either One or Two. The caller (you or a child) calls out a number and a way to move (for example, "Twos hop."). Each child who is a Two moves as indicated to the center of the circle, takes a puzzle piece from the top of the pile and returns using the same movement to his or her partner. If a child takes a piece of the puzzle that the pair does not need, the other child returns it to the pile on the next turn. The caller continues to call numbers and movements until all the puzzle pieces are gone or one pair has put together the whole picture.

Find the Match

Materials: Large index cards, felt pen, scissors, paper bag.

Procedure: What are some things you know about Jesus? (Jesus is God's Son. Jesus never sinned. Jesus healed many people. Jesus taught people about God. Jesus died to take the punishment for our sins. Jesus loves us. Jesus helps us. Jesus is alive!) As children answer, briefly write each answer on a separate index card. Supplement children's answers as needed. Make at least one card for each child. Then give each child a card. Child cuts card into two puzzle pieces (see sketch).

Collect matches from half the group and put matches into the bag. Collect remaining matches and set them aside. Ask children to stand around the perimeter of the room. Each child chooses a card half from the bag. At your signal, children walk around the room to find their matching card halves. After matches are completed, have each pair read the sentence on their card aloud. Help with reading as needed. Repeat with remaining matches.

Easter Reminder

Materials: Easter Reminder Pattern, photocopier, paper, scissors.

Preparation: Photocopy one pattern page for each child and one for yourself. Following the directions at the bottom of the page, make a sample Easter Reminder.

Procedure: How did Jesus show His love for us at Easter? (He died for us. He saved us.) **How can you show that you love Jesus?** (Read the Bible. Say kind words. Help others. Talk to God.) Give each child an Easter Reminder Pattern and scissors. Children cut out patterns and fold them according to the directions at the bottom of the page. To use the reminder, child puts left thumb in the section labeled "1," right thumb in "2," right forefinger in "3" and left forefinger in "4" (see sketch).

Group children in pairs. One child in each pair selects a number from one to four and opens and closes the reminder that number of times. That child chooses a sentence on one of the inner flaps and tells partner a way to show love to Jesus by doing what that sentence says. Then child opens the flap to see the picture inside. Partner then selects a number and follows the same steps as the first child. Repeat as time permits.

Activities • **Lower Elementary** • **Easter Reminder Pattern**

149

Who Saw Him?

Materials: Bibles, pens or pencils, index cards, marker, paper, masking tape or thumbtacks; optional—large sheet of poster board, bright-colored yarn or ribbon.

Preparation: Letter these Bible references on separate index cards: Luke 24:13-35; Luke 24:36-40; John 20:10-16; John 20:24-29; John 21:1-14; Acts 1:1-8; 1 Corinthians 15:6,7. Prepare a card for each child, repeating Bible references as needed. Prepare a bulletin board or large wall space as shown in sketch. (Optional: If bulletin board or wall space is not available, use a large sheet of poster board.)

Procedure: Give each child (or pair of children) a card you prepared and two blank cards. **The Bible reference on your card tells about an event after Jesus rose from the dead. Find and read the Bible refer-**ence on your card. Then, on one blank card, write the names of the people who saw Jesus after He rose. On the other blank card, write a short description of what Jesus did. Children attach cards in a row to bulletin board or wall (or poster board), making sure each card is under the correct heading. (Optional: Provide children with colorful yarn or ribbon to stretch below the cards to make rows.) As children complete this activity, ask such questions as, **How did the people who saw Jesus react? What did they say? What did they do? What do you think you might have done? What did Jesus say to the people He saw? What do you learn about God from the events in the story of Jesus' death and resurrection?**

Easter Traditions

Materials: Markers, length of butcher paper, tape.

Preparation: Letter "Just for Fun" and "Meaningful" on butcher paper as shown in sketch. Tape butcher paper to wall or table-top.

Procedure: Ask for volunteers to name some popular Easter traditions and to tell whether the tradition is just for fun or meaningful. As volunteers answer, list the traditions in the appropriate columns on the butcher paper, leaving space for drawings. **What were your favorite Easter traditions when you were younger? What are your favorite Easter traditions now?**

Children initial traditions they have participated in and draw pictures of the traditions on the butcher paper. Talk with children about Jesus' sacrifice and ways to praise Him. **Which Easter traditions help you think about what it means to say that Jesus is our Savior? If you were to make up a tradition that would help you celebrate what Easter really means, what would it be?**

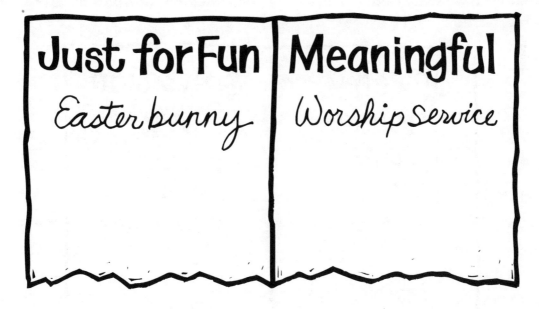

Just for Fun
Easter bunny

Meaningful
Worship Service

Weighing Your Wealth

Materials: Bibles, large sheet of paper, markers.

Preparation: Divide large sheet of paper into two columns.

Procedure: **What are some valuable things that money can buy?** (Jewelry, clothes, toys, games, houses, land, cars, etc.) Have children list their answers in first column of large sheet of paper you prepared.

Easter is the time we focus especially on Jesus' death and resurrection and the gift of salvation. We are going to look at some verses to discover more of the riches that we have from God. Children take turns reading Bible verses to find benefits of the riches God freely gives us as members of His family (John 3:16, Romans 15:13, 2 Thessalonians 2:16, Titus 2:11, Hebrews 4:16, 1 Peter 5:10, 1 John 1:9). Children list these benefits in the second column of large sheet of paper. Use the following questions to lead children in comparing the things that money can buy with the incomparable riches we have in Christ. **Why are the riches God gives us better than anything on earth? When are some times that people might be especially glad to be a member of God's family? Why?**

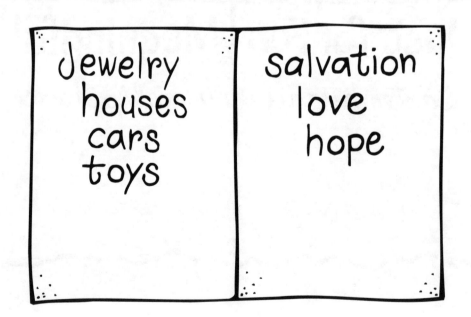

Easter Grace

Materials: None.

Procedure: Children stand in the center of the room. Designate one side of the room "fair" and the other side "foul." Read one of the situations below. Children move to the fair side of the room if they think the person got what was deserved or to the foul side of the room if they don't think the person got what was deserved. Ask a volunteer from each group to tell why he or she thinks that what the person got was deserved (or undeserved).

• Your younger brother gets the same allowance as you, but your parents say it's because he does extra chores.

• Another kid got put in the starting lineup even though she missed practice one day that week, but she didn't come because her mom's car broke down on the way.

• You got an A on a test even though you didn't study.

• You get five dollars for allowance, but your friend only gets two dollars.

Continue the activity, inviting children to think of other situations. **When someone gets what is deserved we call that fair. But sometimes people get good things that they don't deserve. We call that grace. When have you gotten something good you didn't deserve?** Volunteers respond. **What are some things you've received from God that you didn't deserve?** (Love. Kindness. Forgiveness.) **Why don't we deserve God's grace?** (Because we all sin.) **What did God do to show us His grace?** (Sent Jesus to be our Savior. Allowed Jesus to die to take the punishment for our sins.) **The story of Easter is the story of God's grace. How would you tell the Easter story to someone who hadn't heard it before?** Children form pairs and tell each other the story as if the listener hadn't heard the story before.

Whatzit Mean?

Materials: Whatzit Mean? Pattern (double-sided), photocopier, paper, pens or pencils.

Preparation: Photocopy one double-sided Whatzit Mean? Pattern for each child.

Procedure: Distribute Whatzit Mean? Patterns, paper and pens or pencils. **The Easter story tells how God provided us His gift of salvation. These license-plate messages describe that gift. What do the messages say?** Children work in pairs or individually to discover the license-plate messages. (1—undeserved riches, 2—created for good works, 3—can't earn it, 4—God's gift, 5—just forgiven, 6—praise to God.)

How do these messages describe the gift of salvation? Invite children to create their own license-plate messages about salvation or the Easter story, by using a combination of no more than seven letters or numbers. Children trade papers to discover their messages.

WHATZIT MEAN?

FLORIDA FL2000 APR — RICHZ

CALIFORNIA CA2000 APR — UNDSRVD

+

Washington WA2000 APR — GD~WRX

ARIZONA AZ2000 APR — CRE8D4

+

The Hope of Easter

Materials: Masking tape, large container (wastebasket, box or large paper bag), newspaper, jelly beans or other small treats.

Preparation: Make a masking-tape line on the floor approximately 6 feet (1.8 m) from large container.

Procedure: Children crumple sheets of newspaper so that they each have three newspaper "balls." First child stands behind the line and tells how many newspaper balls he or she hopes to be able to toss into the container. Each child gets three tries to toss balls into the container, receiving three jelly beans or other small treats if his or her hopes are realized and one if they aren't.

During or after the activity, talk with children about what it means to have hope.

What are you hoping to do in this activity? What are some other things you hope will happen to you? What can you do to make your hopes come true? Who are you depending on to make your hopes come true? How do you feel when your hopes don't come true? What do you think it means to have hope in a person? (To hope that the person will keep his or her promises.) **What does it mean to have hope in Jesus? What are some ways that He has kept His promises? How does Jesus' death and resurrection help us to hope in Him? What are some things Jesus says He will do in the present and in the future?** Discuss what it means to put our hope in Jesus.

6 feet (1.8 m)

157

Getting Your Hopes Up

Materials: Markers, five sheets of butcher paper, masking tape.

Preparation: Letter each of these questions at the top of separate sheets of butcher paper: "What do you hope to do this summer?" "What do you hope to get for your next birthday?" "What do you hope to have as a career?" "What do you hope to do this week?" "What do you hope to learn to do better?" Tape each sheet of butcher paper to wall or tabletop. Place several markers by each paper.

Procedure: Children write or draw answers to as many questions as they can. Participate in this activity with children, talking with them about their hopes (and yours). After several minutes, call time. **Which of your hopes is LEAST likely to happen? Why? Which of your hopes is MOST likely to happen? Why? Who will make this hope come true? Are you depending on yourself or another person to make this hope come true? Why is it hard sometimes for people to make their hopes come true? In order for our hopes to come true, we have to depend on something or someone to make them come true. Jesus is someone we can all have hope in. What are some reasons that we can hope in Jesus? How does Jesus' death and resurrection help us to hope in Him?**

Praise King Jesus

Materials: Large sheets of butcher paper, markers, tape.

Preparation: Letter each of the following sentences across the top of a separate sheet of paper: "Jesus is the King." "Jesus is God's Son." "He is our Savior." "Praise Him ev'ry-one." Make one paper for each group of two or three children, repeating sentences as necessary.

Procedure: Briefly tell the story of Palm Sunday. Lead children to suggest and discuss reasons people praise Jesus. List reasons on a sheet of paper and tape to wall. Show children the papers with sentences that you prepared. Repeat sentences with children while they keep time with claps and stomps (see sketch). Practice sentences several times so that children are familiar with the rhythm.

Divide class into groups of two or three. Give a different paper to each group. Each group works to write several additional sentences to fit the rhythmic pattern. For ideas, groups may refer to the list on the wall. Gather groups. Each group "performs" its sentence while the rest of the children keep time with claps and stomps.

Where'd It Go?

Materials: Plate, cookies or donuts, large resealable plastic bag, napkins, paper, pens or pencils, large sheet of paper, marker.

Preparation: On the plate, place a few crumbs from the cookies or donuts. Place the cookies or donuts in the plastic bag and hide the bag somewhere in your room. Put the plate and napkins in an obvious place in your room.

Procedure: As children arrive and notice the plate, say, **I brought some (cookies) for us to eat, but they're gone now. What do you think happened to them?** Give children paper and pens or pencils to write down their ideas about what happened to the snack. After a few minutes, ask, **What different ideas did you think of?** (Someone ate them. Early arrivals ate them. An animal came in and ate them.) List children's ideas on large sheet of paper. **Each of your ideas is a theory. A theory is an idea about how and why something has happened. Which of these theories is the most likely explanation for what happened to our snack? How could you prove or disprove one of these theories?** Retrieve snack and serve to children. **After Jesus' body disappeared from the tomb, people—Jesus' disciples and others—thought of several theories about what had happened.** Discuss theories about what happened to Jesus' body. Discuss ways that Jesus prepared His disciples for His death and resurrection. **How did Jesus help His disciples become certain that He had risen from the dead? Why is it important that Jesus died and came back to life?**

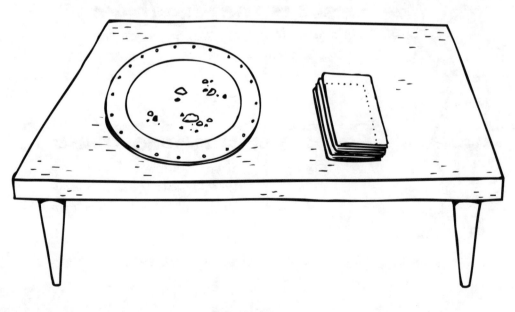

Egg-Carton Holy Week

Materials: Bible, felt pen, small pieces of paper, plastic eggs, symbols of Holy Week—the time from Palm Sunday to Easter (bit of a palm leaf [Matthew 21:1,2,8,9]; piece of wood [Luke 23:26,27]; nail [Matthew 27:33-37,50,51]; stone [Matthew 28:1-6]; etc.), egg carton, large map of Jerusalem and the surrounding area.

Preparation: On small pieces of paper, let-ter Bible references that help to tell the Easter story. Place each reference and a symbol that goes with the reference in an egg. Put the eggs in story order in the egg carton.

Procedure: Children take turns opening the eggs. As each egg is opened, help child read the Scripture and let child tell that portion of the story. Child then places symbol on map to show where each event took place.

Krazy Kapers

Materials: Krazy Kapers Pattern (double-sided), photocopier, paper, pens or pencils.

Preparation: Photocopy one double-sided Krazy Kapers Pattern for each child.

Procedure: Children form pairs. Give each child a Krazy Kapers Pattern and a pen or pencil. Doing one Kaper at a time, each child fills in the blanks by asking his or her partner to name an example of what is needed. For example, to begin Kaper #1, child asks his or her partner to name a piece of furniture; child then writes on the blank line the piece of furniture named by his or her partner. Child continues in this same manner until all the blanks are filled in. Then the partner completes the other Kaper in the same manner. (You may choose to have all children complete both Kapers or have each child complete one Kaper and take home the other Kaper to complete with a family member.) Invite pairs to share one of their Kapers with the whole group.

Who had to sacrifice what in these stories? Which sacrifice would be the hardest? Why? Have you or someone you know ever made one of these sacrifices? When have you had to sacrifice, or give up, something? Was it hard or easy? What were the results of your sacrifice? "Sacrifice" is a word used in the Bible to describe what God gave for our benefit. What did God sacrifice for us? Discuss the meaning of this sacrifice with children.

#1

Yesterday I woke up in my _____ (adjective) allergies. I sounded like a _____ (furniture) with _____. My eyes watered and my skin (animal) got puffy with _____ (color) spots. My friends all thought that I was _____ (adjective). My mother took me to the doctor. The doctor said I had a virus and the _____ temperature was _____ (sickness) and my (number). Then the doctor said I couldn't eat broccoli, squash or _____ (color) anymore. But I could eat pizza and _____ (food) and eggplant all the time. Then the doctor asked if I had a (candy) cat. I said, "Yes, my cat likes to _____ (action)." The doctor said I would have to sacrifice and give my cat away. I felt _____ (feeling). But I gave my cat to my friend, _____ (name). My friend was very happy. My mother said that I could have a _____ (color) _____ (name of dinosaur) instead.

My name is _____ . I am on the _____ [name of animal]
baseball team. Our game was on Monday at [name]
_____ . It was a _____ day. The game was [time] [weather]
tied at _____ runs. In the last game [number]
I had hit _____ home runs. Now we had a [number]
runner on first base. Then the batter before
me struck out! I wanted to hit the ball to
_____ . But the coach told me to sacrifice! [place]
Me—the best hitter on the team—sacrifice?
I felt _____ . I hit a _____ -foot bunt [feeling] [number]
toward third base. The third base man
picked up the ball, but threw it into
_____ . Meanwhile the guy on first base [place]
ran all the way to home. The crowds
_____ ! The coach said I did a great job [action]
and took us all out for _____ and _____ [food] [drink]
in a _____ . [car]

Word Connections

Materials: Bibles, large sheet of paper, markers in a variety of colors, paper, pens or pencils.

Procedure: Have children locate John 10:14-17 in their Bibles. Ask a volunteer to read the passage aloud. **How is Jesus like a shepherd to us?** (Loves us. Guides us. Helps us. Forgives us.) **What does a good shepherd do for his sheep?** (Lays down his life for them.) **What did Jesus do for us?** (Died on the cross.) **What did Jesus mean when He said, "I lay down my life—only to take it up again"?** (Jesus died, but He rose again.)

Draw a large circle on large sheet of paper. Ask children to suggest words related to John 10:14-17. Letter words on paper around edge of large circle. Supplement children's suggestions as needed.

Group children into pairs. Each pair chooses any two words and writes a sentence that uses the two words and tells something about how Jesus is like a shepherd to us. After several minutes, invite a volunteer to read aloud the sentence the pair created. Draw a line connecting the two words used in the sentence. Continue the activity, using as many different colors as possible to draw connecting lines as each pair reads its sentence aloud.

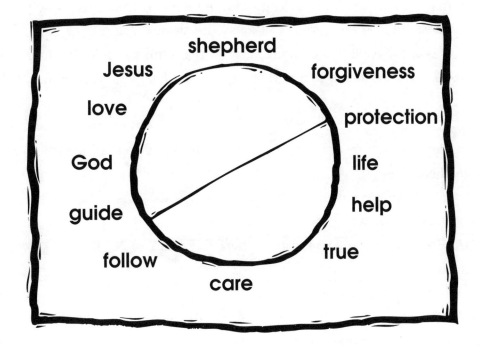

Activities • **Upper Elementary**

He's Alive!

CHARACTERS

MARY MAGDALENE

MARY (MOTHER OF JESUS)

JOANNA

PETER

JOHN

ANGEL

JESUS

SCENE ONE

MARY MAGDALENE: So? How are we going to do it?

MARY: I don't know.

JOANNA: It's a very heavy stone.

MARY MAGDALENE: Maybe if we all push together?

MARY: Don't be silly.

JOANNA: Maybe the guards will help us.

MARY: Maybe, maybe, maybe. We should go and get some of the men to help us. Four of the stronger ones should be enough to roll away the stone.

MARY MAGDALENE: No way! If the guards saw so many men coming, you know what would happen. They'd attack first and ask questions later. But maybe they'll help three women.

JOANNA: Why wouldn't they? We're only going to make sure that the body is properly buried. They'll be there the whole time. It's not like we're going to steal anything.

MARY MAGDALENE: Well, maybe they'll help.

MARY: It's the only hope we have.

JOANNA: Are we almost there?

MARY MAGDALENE: Of course. You know where the tomb is.

MARY: It's right over there.

JOANNA: But where are the guards?

MARY MAGDALENE: And why is the stone over on the side and not in front of the entrance?

MARY: There's something strange going on here.

JOANNA: The body's gone!

MARY MAGDALENE: I'd better go and tell Peter and John. *(She runs off.)*

MARY: Should we go in?

JOANNA: It's awfully dark.

MARY: But we must know what happened.

JOANNA: But it's awfully dark.

MARY: No it's not. It's light. Where did the light come from?

ANGEL: Who is it that you seek?

MARY AND JOANNA: Who are you, sir? And why do you shine?

ANGEL: I am an angel of the Lord. Why do you seek for the living among the dead? Do you not remember that He said evil men would kill Him, but on the third day, He would rise again?

MARY: Are you telling us that He's alive?

JOANNA: Just as He said in Galilee. I remember.

ANGEL: Go to the disciples and tell them the good news. He's alive.

MARY AND JOANNA: We will! We will! *(They run off.)*

SCENE TWO

PETER: Who's banging on the door?

MARY MAGDALENE *(gasping for breath)*: Mary.

PETER: Who?

JOHN: She said, "Mary."

PETER: It could be a trick. Mary who?

MARY MAGDALENE *(gasping for breath)*: Mary…*(Gasps.)* Magdalene.

JOHN: It sounds like her. Let her in.

PETER: OK. You're in. What is it?

MARY MAGDALENE *(gasping for breath)*: Jesus. Tomb. Stone. Gone. Body.

JOHN: Whoa. Whoa. Whoa.

PETER: Pull in your nets, woman. Take a deep breath and start over.

JOHN: You're not making any sense.

MARY MAGDALENE: We went to Jesus' tomb.

PETER: Why'd you do that?

MARY MAGDALENE: To anoint His body. To give it a proper burial.

JOHN: Well that was dumb. How are you women going to move that stone?

MARY MAGDALENE: We didn't have to. It was already moved.

PETER: Sure it was. With guards all around the tomb.

MARY MAGDALENE: I'm telling you. It was rolled away from the entrance.

JOHN: You must have gone to the wrong place.

MARY MAGDALENE: No, we didn't. Go! See for yourselves.

PETER: We will! C'mon, John.

JOHN: Just far enough to see the guards.

PETER: Well, of course. No point in getting killed because some hysterical women can't find the right tomb.

MARY MAGDALENE: We were at the right place! Somebody's taken the body.

JOHN: Sure they did. Let's go and see, Peter. *(They run off to the tomb.)*

PETER *(puffing while jogging)*: It looks peaceful enough so far.

JOHN *(also puffing)*: Try to keep up! But be quiet. We don't want to alert the guards.

PETER: I am being quiet. Just over this hill, we'll see the tomb. Don't get so far ahead.

JOHN: I can see the tomb.

PETER: And?

JOHN: I can see the stone.

PETER: And?

JOHN: I can't see the guards.

PETER: What?

JOHN: I can't see the guards. They're not there.

PETER: What? Let me see. What's the stone doing way over there?

JOHN: I don't know.

PETER: Where are you going?

JOHN: To get a better look. C'mon.

PETER: Well, slow down. Don't go running into danger.

JOHN: What danger?

PETER: How do I know? But something strange is happening.

JOHN: C'mon. Maybe Mary was right.

PETER: Slow down. OK, you got here first and you're blocking the entrance. So what do you see?

JOHN: Nothing.

PETER: What do you mean, "nothing"? Get out of the way.

JOHN: Well, you don't have to push.

PETER: Look. Look at the burial cloths!

JOHN: What about them?

PETER: They're still completely wrapped. Just like the body floated out of them. Whoever did this was certainly neat.

JOHN: Something's wrong.

PETER: What do you mean?

JOHN: Where's the headpiece?

PETER: I don't know. Must have been taken with the body.

JOHN: But why? Why would anybody steal a body with the headpiece and then rewrap the linen cloths?

PETER: They didn't.

JOHN: What?

PETER: They didn't take the headpiece. It's wrapped up over here in the corner.

JOHN: What? Peter! He's alive! He must be.

PETER: What are you talking about?

JOHN: Jesus is alive! It's the only thing that makes sense!

PETER: He's dead. You saw Him crucified. You saw the spear in His side.

JOHN: But nobody would rob a grave this way. He's alive, I tell you!

PETER: Maybe. I want to study this some more. Let's go.

JOHN: But He's alive! We have to tell the others.

PETER: Just keep quiet. Dead people don't come back to life.

JOHN: What about Lazarus?

PETER: Just keep quiet and let me think. *(They leave for home.)*

SCENE THREE

MARY MAGDALENE *(sobbing softly)***:** Why? Why? Why?

ANGEL: Why do you weep?

MARY MAGDALENE: Because somebody took away my Lord. And I don't know where they put Him. *(She sinks to her knees and covers her face with her hands.)*

JESUS: Woman, why do you weep?

MARY MAGDALENE *(sobbing)***:** Sir?

JESUS: Whom do you seek?

MARY MAGDALENE: Sir, if you are the gardener and took away my Lord, please tell me where to find Him. Let me take Him to another place so that we can visit His grave.

JESUS: Mary.

MARY MAGDALENE: *(Looks up, amazed.)* Master?

JESUS: Go and tell My brothers that I am going back to My Father and your Father—to My God and your God.

MARY MAGDALENE: I will. I will. *(She gets up.)* He's alive! He's alive!

(This and other Bible skits can be found in the reproducible *The Big Book of Bible Skits* from Gospel Light.)

Going Fishing

CHARACTERS

PETER

THOMAS

NATHANAEL

PETER: Thomas! Nathanael! I'm going fishing. Are you two coming or not?

THOMAS: Sounds good to me.

NATHANAEL: I'm in, Peter. Have you got a spot in mind?

PETER: What kind of dumb question is that, Nathanael? I always pick good spots.

THOMAS: James! John! And you other two! C'mon! Peter says he knows a good place to go fishing.

NATHANAEL: Looks like we're all coming, Peter. But level with me. You're not planning to go back to fishing, are you?

PETER: No, I don't think so. But I need a place to think. And the sea is as good a place as any. C'mon, Thomas! Hurry up!

THOMAS: We're here, Peter. Don't be so impatient. The fish aren't going anywhere.

NATHANAEL: Don't be too hard on him, Thomas. He says he wants to think. And you know how tough THAT is for him.

PETER: Some friend you are. C'mon! Let's move the boat out toward the east.

THOMAS: OK, Peter. We're underway. While we're heading toward your fishing spot, tell us what's on your mind. Sometimes it helps to think out loud.

PETER: I was thinking about the supper we had with Jesus.

THOMAS: Give us a break. Which one? We had lots of suppers with Him.

NATHANAEL: Don't pretend to be so dense, Thomas. The last one.

PETER: That's the one, Nathanael. And this is the best fishing spot in Galilee. Help me toss the net in, Nathanael. *(Pauses.)* Do you remember when Jesus washed our feet?

NATHANAEL: That would be pretty hard to forget.

THOMAS: Especially for you, Peter. Your quick tongue got you in trouble again.

PETER: Maybe it did, Thomas. But I had a reason for what I said and did. At least I didn't just sit there like a bump on a log and not understand what was happening.

NATHANAEL: Would you two stop arguing with each other? What's bothering you now, Peter?

PETER: Do you remember how you felt when Jesus got out the basin and the cloth and began washing our feet?

THOMAS: Of course. I was totally dumbfounded. I didn't know what to do or say. So I just sat there and let Him wash my feet.

NATHANAEL: So what do you need to think about now, Peter? Jesus explained that He was setting an example for us to follow. He washed our feet so that we should be willing to wash each other's feet.

THOMAS: Sure. It was a simple lesson. If the master could humble Himself before His servants, then the servants can humble themselves before each other.

PETER: But here's the problem. Do you think He meant just us twelve—or eleven? Or do you think He meant we should be servants to anyone?

THOMAS: Peter, you surely do have a habit of complicating everything. We're to be the leaders of His Church on earth. Why would we be required to be servants of everyone who comes along?

PETER: That's what I thought, at first. But...do any of you doubt that He's the Messiah?

THOMAS: Not after I saw the nail holes in His hands and the gash in His side. Why do you ask?

PETER: Well, if He's the Messiah—and He is—then that means God Himself washed our feet. If He could stoop so low, how could we feel that we don't have to serve others in the same manner?

NATHANAEL: You've got a point there.

THOMAS: I think we should have a rule that Peter isn't allowed to think anymore. Every time he does, something I've just decided goes out the window. Besides, when he thinks, he loses his memory. I thought you said this was a good place to fish?

PETER: So excuse me for living. Didn't you ever have a day when you didn't catch anything before?

THOMAS: Not when somebody told me he had the best fishing spot in Israel.

NATHANAEL: Can't you two stop bickering?

PETER: I see we're not the only people out this early in the morning.

THOMAS: What do you mean?

PETER: Look. Over there on the shore. Some guy's out for a walk.

NATHANAEL: So what's he doing?

PETER: He's just standing there. Watching us.

NATHANAEL: So who is it? Do we know him?

THOMAS: It's hard to say. The light's not very good yet and it's mostly in our eyes.

PETER: Listen. The guy on the shore shouted something. He wants to know if we caught anything.

NATHANAEL: Well, isn't anyone going to answer him? We can still be civilized, even if we did have a bad night's fishing.

THOMAS: Let Peter do it. He has the biggest mouth.

PETER: Just to show how civilized I can be, I'm going to ignore that last crack. *(Shouts.)* No! We haven't caught anything. *(Speaks normally.)* Typical landlubber. He says we should try the other side of the boat. What's he think? That fish have a fence they can't cross over?

NATHANAEL: Well? What have we got to lose? The net's ready to cast again anyway. We can troll to shore and if we catch something, we won't have wasted a night. If we don't catch anything, we can teach the landlubber how to fold a net.

PETER: If you want to waste your time, go ahead. *(THOMAS and NATHANAEL cast net.)*

THOMAS: Hey! What's happening to the boat?

NATHANAEL: Well, I'll be! It's being pulled to one side by the weight of the fish in the net!

PETER: We'll have to row to shore. We'll never pull the nets in with this many fish in them!

THOMAS: Who is that guy on the shore?

NATHANAEL: I don't know. But he sure knows his fishing.

PETER: It's the Lord! It has to be!

THOMAS: Peter! What are you doing? Look at that! He jumps in the water to swim to shore and leaves the six of us to handle all these fish by ourselves. And he has the GALL to talk about being a servant!

(This and other Bible skits can be found in the reproducible *The Big Book of Bible Skits* from Gospel Light.)

I Will Return

CHARACTERS
CAPTAIN
SOLDIERS

CAPTAIN (*closing up duffle bag*)**:** Well, men, the time has come. I'll be leaving shortly.

SOLDIER ONE: Don't go, sir.

SOLDIER TWO: We need you here.

SOLDIER THREE: It just won't seem like home without you.

CAPTAIN: It's not SUPPOSED to seem like home—It ISN'T home!

SOLDIER THREE: Oh, yeah. I forgot. We've been here for so long.

SOLDIER ONE: Can't we come with you, sir?

SOLDIER TWO: Yeah, please take us with you.

CAPTAIN: I can't. There's still a lot to do here. I'm counting on you to do it.

SOLDIER ONE: Yes, sir.

SOLDIER TWO: Whatever you say, sir.

SOLDIER THREE: We'll do our duty, sir.

CAPTAIN: Good men. I knew when I chose you that you would be faithful.

SOLDIERS (*saluting*)**:** Yes, sir!

CAPTAIN: Now, here's the plan. I'll be leaving as soon as the chopper gets here.

SOLDIER ONE: You need someone to clear away the undergrowth for you, sir?

SOLDIER TWO: Someone with a machete?

SOLDIER THREE: Choose me, sir. I can do it.

CAPTAIN: Chopper. Helicopter.

SOLDIERS (*to each other*)**:** I knew that.

CAPTAIN: There is one important thing to remember. I'm leaving now, but I will return.

SOLDIER ONE: You will?

SOLDIER TWO: When?

SOLDIER THREE: Will there be some kind of special signal?

CAPTAIN: Many things will happen before I return.

SOLDIER ONE: What kind of things, sir?

CAPTAIN: You will hear rumors of battles around you.

SOLDIER TWO: Check.

CAPTAIN: You will see battles happening around you.

SOLDIER THREE: Check.

CAPTAIN: There will be hardships—hunger, disease, earthquakes.

SOLDIER ONE: Check.

CAPTAIN: But I'm counting on you to remain true to your allegiance.

SOLDIERS: Check!

CAPTAIN: Before my return, many will be disheartened.

SOLDIER ONE: Not us.

CAPTAIN: No, not you three.

SOLDIER TWO: What do we do about the others?

CAPTAIN: Encourage them. Support them in their times of weakness.

SOLDIER THREE: But, sir, how will we have the strength?

CAPTAIN: I'm not leaving you alone. You'll have the radio.

SOLDIER ONE: Begging your pardon, sir, but how will that help us?

CAPTAIN: Good question. A lieutenant will be monitoring the radio day and night. He will be in contact with me. If you ever need help, call.

SOLDIER TWO: We will, sir.

CAPTAIN: When I return, I'll be coming by air.

SOLDIER THREE: We'll watch for you every day, sir.

CAPTAIN: No, you won't.

SOLDIERS: We won't?

CAPTAIN: No. You'll be busy. I expect you to do the things we've been doing.

SOLDIER ONE: You mean like helping the sick?

SOLDIER TWO: Feeding the hungry?

SOLDIER THREE: Saving the nation from its oppressors?

CAPTAIN: That's right. *(Lifts backpack to shoulder.)* Carry on.

SOLDIER ONE: But, Captain. Before you go—WHY must you go?

CAPTAIN: I'm heading out to prepare the new headquarters. When your tour of duty is finished, there'll be a place for you there.

SOLDIER TWO: But how do we know that for sure?

CAPTAIN: Because I'm telling you. Would I say it if it were false?

SOLDIER THREE: No, sir. You've never lied to us. But can't you give us some idea of when you'll be back?

CAPTAIN: No, because I don't know myself. One last warning...

SOLDIERS: Yes, sir?

CAPTAIN: The enemy will send many false signals, telling you they're from me. They may even send an impersonator.

SOLDIER ONE: How will we know if a message is from you, sir?

CAPTAIN: Have I ever wavered in my orders?

SOLDIER TWO: No, sir. You've always been the same.

CAPTAIN: Test any new orders against my old ones. If they're in conflict, I did not send them.

SOLDIER THREE: How will we know if you've come back or if it's an impersonator?

CAPTAIN: You will all see me. If anyone comes and says he's seen me, don't believe him. I will show myself to all of you when I return. There's my ride. I have to go now.

SOLDIER ONE: Good-bye, sir.

SOLDIER TWO: We'll be waiting for you.

SOLDIER THREE: But while we wait, we'll be obeying your orders, sir. *(SOLDIERS salute; CAPTAIN returns salute.)*

CAPTAIN: As you were. *(CAPTAIN exits. SOLDIERS slowly raise their heads as they watch helicopter take off. ALL salute.)*

(This and other Bible skits can be found in the reproducible *The Big Book of Bible Skits* from Gospel Light.)

ALLELUIA!

Stories

Story Tips

Storytelling has been a popular and effective teaching method for centuries. Everyone loves to hear a good story, especially if it's a TRUE story. And that is what is so wonderful about these Easter stories written by Ethel Barrett—all that happens in them happened to real people and each story is full of captivating word pictures and dramatic action. These are just the sort of stories that demand to be read aloud and that will capture the interest of children of all ages! The following tips will help you read the stories with more confidence and greater effect, so your listening audience will be able to get the full benefit of what the Easter story means.

• Practice reading the stories ahead of time, even if it's only in front of a mirror.
• Use your normal speaking voice. Avoid talking down to children or making the story sound like either a fairy tale or a solemn declaration. Read clearly, distinctly and slowly, but avoid the tones and mannerisms people often adopt when talking to someone they think cannot hear or understand.
• Try whispering when you come to a crucial point in the narrative. A whisper is the most dramatic sound the human voice can utter.
• Vary your speaking rate—speeding up or slowing down—in order to convey importance or secure attention. An occasional pause is very effective in creating suspense.
• Add sound effects where appropriate.
• Add gestures when they fit.
• Put yourself in the place of the characters and speak (and even act) as they would.
• Use facial expressions to convey emotions. Smile when referring to good things. Look angry or frightened or sad when that is how a story character might have felt.

(These tips are adapted from Gospel Light's *Everything You Want to Know About Teaching Young Children, Birth-6 Years.*)

An Exciting Day in Jerusalem (Palm Sunday)

Matthew 21:1-11; Mark 11:1-10; Luke 19:29-38

The disciples had no way of knowing what an exciting day this was going to be. It started out just like any other day.

Early in the morning, Jesus and His disciples left the little village where they had been staying. It was ordinary enough—just Jesus and His disciples. As they walked along the road, people began to join them. The day was quiet and bright and blue. The disciples hardly noticed the excitement at first. They could just sort of FEEL it beginning.

It began when Jesus asked two of His disciples to go ahead to the next village and get a donkey. "Not just ANY donkey," He told them. "There's a CERTAIN donkey. Untie him and bring him to Me."

The disciples went to the village, and it was exactly as Jesus had said. They brought the donkey back to Jesus, and that was when the excitement began to grow a little.

Some of the people took off their bright-colored robes and folded them across the donkey's back for Jesus to sit on. Now Jesus looked like a KING as He went down the road toward Jerusalem. And more and more people began to follow along—old people, young people and CHILDREN.

And the excitement began to grow a little more.

Somebody took off his robe and spread it on the ground in front of Jesus. Then somebody else did. And then somebody else did, too.

Then people began to cut branches from palm trees.They waved the branches in the air and spread them on the road.

The road was just covered with bright-colored robes and more bright-colored robes and branches and branches and more branches.

Now a sight like that was too exciting for people to keep to themselves. The news spread ahead to Jerusalem. And when Jesus and His disciples got to the gates of Jerusalem, it seemed like EVERYBODY was out to meet them! And the excitement grew and burst out like great swelling MUSIC.

People were packed on both sides of the streets—the children in front so they could see.

And the people threw flowers.

And they spread out leaves.

And they waved palm branches.

And they SANG!

They sang, "Hosanna in the highest! Blessed is He who comes in the name of the Lord!"

And from the city gates to the great

Temple with its golden roof, that song was in the air. The children sang it in the streets. They sang it in the Temple courts. They filled the air with it. It was one of the most exciting days they'd ever had in Jerusalem.

The old people and young people and children all wanted Jesus to know how much they loved Him! And they TOLD Him so!

LET'S TALK ABOUT THE BIBLE STORY

Can you think of all the different ways you can praise God in Sunday School? in church? Can you name some ways you can praise Him during the week?

A BIBLE VERSE TO LEARN

Sing to the Lord with thanksgiving. (Psalm 147:7)

LET'S TALK TO GOD

Dear God, we ARE thankful for You. You are so good to us! Help us to do what You want us to do—not only on Sunday but also every day in the week. We know that this is one way we can praise You. In Jesus' name, amen.

The Saddest Day (Good Friday)

Mark 15:1-47; Luke 23:33-49

Oh, that was a glad day, when Jesus rode into Jerusalem on the donkey and people spread their robes on the ground and waved palm branches and the children sang and sang until the music seemed to rise to the very skies! It seemed absolutely impossible that anything dreadful could happen after such a glad day.

But it did.

It all began with some people who did not believe that Jesus is the Son of God. It would have been quite dreadful enough if they just didn't believe it and let it go at that. But they didn't stop there. They sent a band of soldiers after Jesus. And the soldiers caught Him in a garden where He was praying to God. And they arrested Him and dragged Him before the ruler. And the ruler had Him tied to a post and whipped. It would have been dreadful enough if they had stopped THERE. But they did not.

When the ruler asked the people what they wanted to do with Jesus, some people cried out, "Kill him!" Then MORE people cried out, "KILL HIM!" They cried it out louder and louder and LOUDER, until there was such confusion and noise and shouting that it seemed to rise to the very skies, just the way the singing had done on that excit-

ing day when Jesus road into Jerusalem!

But this was different from the singing. This was different from the glad, exciting day.

The people who didn't believe in Jesus made a big wooden cross. They dragged Jesus into the street. They made Him carry the cross through the city. They took Him to a hill just outside the city. And there, on that hill, they nailed Him by His hands and His feet to the cross. And they put the cross in a hole in the ground, so it stood up straight and tall. And there they left Him to die.

It seemed incredible! Jesus was dead! It was just so hard to believe! JESUS was dead!

It was all over. All the gladness was over.

His friends took Him down from the cross. They carried Him—oh so tenderly—to a garden tomb. And there they wrapped Him in soft clean cloths. And there they left Him.

The soldiers rolled a HUGE stone over the door of the tomb. And Jesus' friends felt that there was no more gladness, anywhere in the world, anymore.

It was the saddest day in the world. But little did they know that there was a GLAD day coming! And it was just around the corner! The GLADDEST day in the world was coming!

Stories • **All Ages**

LET'S TALK ABOUT THE BIBLE STORY

Everything seems to be in a hopeless state. But do you know why Jesus left His home in heaven and came to earth to die on the cross? He did this because He LOVES you! He did this to make a way for us to be forgiven for the wrong things we do. This is what the Bible means when it says that Jesus Christ came to be your Savior. Believe it! Let Him KNOW you believe it! It's the most wonderful news in the world!

A BIBLE VERSE TO LEARN

God so loved the world [that means you] *that he gave his one and only Son, that whoever* [that means you again] *believes in him shall...have eternal life.* (John 3:16)

LET'S TALK TO GOD

Dear God, we know that from the beginning of the world You planned to have Jesus die for us. And when the time came, it happened, just as You planned it. We thank Jesus for doing this. And we thank YOU for loving us so much that You sent us a Savior. In Jesus' name, amen.

The Gladdest Day (Easter)

Matthew 28:1-20; Mark 16:1-15; Luke 24:1-12

The day started out to be sad. It was still the saddest time in the world for Jesus' friends. Some of them were SO sad that they got up early in the morning and hurried back to the tomb in the garden where they had left Him—the tomb with the stone rolled in front of it. They knew it was all over and He was dead. But they had spices and sweet perfumes for Him, and they hoped they would find someone to roll the stone away.

They hurried to the garden, and actually that's all they expected to see: a tomb with a huge stone rolled over the doorway. But when they got there, the great stone door of the tomb had been rolled away! And Jesus was GONE!

At first they just stood there, STUNNED.

And then they all did different things.

One of them turned on her heels and ran. Her name was Mary Magdalene. And she wasn't just running away. She was running to tell two other special friends.

The rest of them went into the tomb, and—surprise of all surprises!—there were two ANGELS inside!

Jesus' friends just stood there, absolutely speechless. They couldn't say a thing.

ANGELS!

And before Jesus' friends could find their voices, the angels said, "He is not dead. He is alive. He is RISEN—just as He told you He would be."

Well, first Jesus' friends just stood there, stunned. And then THEY turned on THEIR heels and ran, just as Mary Magdalene had done.

Then the garden was quiet.

But it wasn't quiet for long.

First, the two special friends Mary Magdalene had run to tell came back. One of them stood and looked in the tomb. The other one went right inside. And sure enough, everything Mary had told them was true. The cloths Jesus had been wrapped in were there, all neat and in order, and the cloth that had been wrapped around His head was folded neatly. But HE was gone. They went out of the garden, AMAZED.

Then the garden was quiet again.

But it wasn't quiet for long.

For last of all, Mary Magdalene came back. And she stood there by the tomb. And she cried.

"Why are you crying?" asked the angels.

And Mary said, "Because I do not know where Jesus is."

And then, suddenly, she realized that there was somebody standing just behind

her. She turned around. It was a man; but in the early morning half-darkness, she did not know Him. She thought perhaps He might be the gardener.

"Why are you crying? He asked. "And who are you looking for?"

"Oh," said Mary, "I'm looking for Jesus. Do YOU know where they have taken Him?"

And the stranger said softly—oh so softly and lovingly—"Mary." Just like that.

And the MINUTE He said her name— "Mary"—she knew who He was.

It was JESUS! He was alive! Oh, joy!

"Jesus!" said Mary. It couldn't be true. But it WAS. He was standing right there. He was looking at her. And He SPOKE to her again.

"Go tell My friends that I'm alive," He said, "and that I'm going to heaven—just as I said I would."

And she did!

Oh, it was a GLAD day after all! It was a VERY GLAD day! It was the GLADDEST day in the world!

Do you know what?
It was the first EASTER SUNDAY!

LET'S TALK ABOUT THE BIBLE STORY

Jesus is alive today—the BIBLE tells us so. He is with us, in our hearts. How can we talk to Him? How can we listen to Him speaking to us? Can you think of some of the many ways He helps you in your own life?

A BIBLE VERSE TO LEARN

I am with you always, to the very end of the age. (Matthew 28:20)

LET'S TALK TO GOD

Dear God, how we thank You that when we sing the words "Jesus loves me; this I know, for the Bible tells me so," it isn't just a lot of WORDS. The Bible DOES tell us so, and it's all true. How wonderful it is that Jesus is alive and we can talk to each other. We appreciate this, God. And we thank You. In Jesus' name, amen.

The Best News! (Ascension)

Mark 16:12-20; Luke 24:13-53; Acts 1:1-12

Yes, Easter was the gladdest day in the world. Jesus had come out of the tomb alive. Mary had seen Him. And she had run to tell all His friends, just as He had asked her to.

And after that they saw Him—not every day as they used to—but at the most surprising times!

One time two of them were just walking along the road on their way to a town called Emmaus, and there He was, walking along the road!

One time some of them just got back from fishing all night, and there He was, on the shore!

One time some of them were gathered together in a room in Jerusalem, and there He was, right in the room!

And then, ONE time they were with Him on the top of a mountain when, suddenly, Jesus began to rise up into the air, right before their very eyes! Up—up—UP—until a big cloud covered Him up and He was GONE!

Why they just stood there staring at the sky. They were absolutely SPEECHLESS. And while they were staring, two angels suddenly stood right alongside them!

"Why are you staring up into heaven?"

the two angels asked. "Jesus is coming back again. Don't you remember? He's coming back again exactly the same way you just saw Him go—through the clouds!"

And then they DID remember.

Of course!

Jesus had told them a long, LONG time ago that He was going away. And they had been so sad.

"Going away?" they had said. "Going AWAY? OH, NO!" And then they had all talked at once. "We will go with you," they had said.

And Jesus had looked at their sad faces, and oh, His eyes had been so KIND. "You cannot go with me NOW," He said. "But SOMEDAY, you can."

Ahhhhh... SOMEDAY, they had thought. And then they had wanted to know where He was going and what the place He was going to was LIKE.

And He had said to them, "I'm going to get a new home ready for you. It will be more beautiful than this world, more beautiful than anything you have ever SEEN or anything you could even IMAGINE." And He had gone on to tell them about heaven, where no one will ever be sick and no one will ever cry and no one will ever be unhappy. "And

someday you can come and live there with me forever," He had said.

Of course!

They remembered; they remembered!

They couldn't be with Him NOW. But SOMEDAY....

They remembered; they remembered!

And they ran and ran to tell all the people!

LET'S TALK ABOUT THE BIBLE STORY

Everything in the Bible is according to God's plan. He made the world, and it was JUST RIGHT. He planned for Jesus to be born, and He WAS. He planned for Jesus to die for us, and He DID. He planned for Jesus to rise again, and He DID. He planned for Jesus to go back up to heaven and prepare a place for us, and He DID. And He plans for Jesus to come again, and He WILL! Isn't that all good news? And shouldn't you run and run and tell all the people?

A BIBLE VERSE TO LEARN

I will come back and take you to be with me that you also may be where I am. (John 14:3)

LET'S TALK TO GOD

Dear God, we thank You that we can be with You someday in heaven. Help us to love You and tell others about You while we're waiting. In Jesus' name, amen.

The First Easter

What's Easter like in your family? Do you wear new clothes or, maybe, new shoes? Anyhow, new clothes or not, do you get all scrubbed and dressed up and go to Sunday School and church?

Do you think the very first Easter was like that?

You do?

You DON'T?

Well, what do you think the very first Easter WAS like? Do you think it was happy?

Well, it turned OUT happy.

But the whole story didn't START OUT that way. It started out very sad, for Jesus was dead. His enemies had dragged Him through the streets of Jerusalem, to a hill just outside the city. And they had nailed Him by His hands and feet to a cross. And they had put the cross in a great big hole dug in the ground, so the cross would stand up straight. And they had left Him to die.

Afterward, His friends had taken Him down from the cross and wrapped Him in clean cloths and tenderly carried Him to a garden tomb outside the city. This tomb was just like a cave. It was carved in the rocky hillside.

Then soldiers had rolled an ENORMOUS stone over the entrance and stayed there to guard the tomb. And all of Jesus' disciples had gone back to the city and gathered together in a room and locked the door, so they could hide. They were frightened.

One day went by.

Two days went by.

And at the end of the second day, one by one, the lights went out in all the houses in the city. And everything was dark. The garden where the tomb was, was dark, too. The flowers had folded up their petals and gone to sleep for the night. Even the leaves on the trees were quiet. Nothing stirred. Not a leaf rustled. The birds had long ago tucked themselves in and were fast asleep.

The guards were outside the tomb, some of them standing and some of them sitting on the ground.

It was quiet, quiet, quiet.

Then SUDDENLY, the earth began to tremble!

The soldiers got to their feet!

And then, in a twinkling of an eye, an angel of the Lord came down from heaven! With the speed of sound he came and seemed to split the sky! His face shone like lightning! His clothing was a brilliant white! And before the horrified eyes of the soldiers, he went up to the great stone that closed

the tomb. And he touched the stone. And his strength was so great that with a little push, he ROLLED IT ASIDE!

It was open! THE TOMB WAS OPEN!

The soldiers fell back, shaking with fear.

And the angel looked at them, just LOOKED at them, and they fell down like dead men!

Then it was all quiet again.

And then, slowly, the darkness began to go away. It got brighter. And the birds in their nests raised their heads and began stirring about. And the flowers began to unfold their petals. It was early morning.

And then the sound of voices! Women's voices! There was Mary, the mother of James, and Mary Magdalene and Joanna and Salome and some others, too. They had spices and perfumes with them for Jesus. And they hoped they'd find somebody to roll the stone away.

They came closer and closer, until they got to the garden. And then they stopped.

The tomb was open! The tomb was OPEN! The great stone was rolled aside! And Jesus was gone! And then two angels appeared, right before their eyes!

The women just stood there as if they were stuck to the ground. They couldn't move.

"Don't be afraid," the angels said.

The women couldn't move.

"He is alive. He is RISEN," the angels said.

Still the women couldn't move.

"He is RISEN," the angels went on, "just as He told you He would be."

This time the women MOVED.

First Mary Magdalene ran. Then the others ran. They all RAN back to the city.

And they told the disciples all about what had happened. And do you know WHAT?

The disciples didn't believe it! "Ha," they said, "you're telling fairy tales!"

But two of the disciples decided to go see for themselves. Their names were Peter and John.

They huffed and puffed all the way back to the garden tomb.

Then they stopped in their tracks.

The women were right.

The stone HAD been rolled away!

They went up to the entrance.

First they PEEKED in.

And then Peter STEPPED in—right inside the tomb. And sure enough, Jesus was gone. The cloths He had been wrapped in were there, right before Peter's eyes, all neat and in order. And the cloth that had been wrapped around His head was there too, all folded up neatly.

Peter came out and he and John stared at each other in amazement. And they walked back to the city in wonder. Jesus was gone. But WHERE? HOW? They couldn't imagine!

All day the disciples wondered. And they not only wondered, but they were also

AFRAID. And they weren't just a LITTLE BIT afraid. They were so afraid that they got together in a big room and locked the door.

The morning went by.

The afternoon went by.

And the evening came. And they ate their supper. And that's when it happened.

Suddenly, right there, before their very eyes, was JESUS!

Yes, He WAS, or WAS He? The doors were locked. How did He get in ? Or was He a GHOST?!

They backed away, TERRIFIED.

And then He spoke to them!

"Why are you afraid?" He said. "I am really Jesus. Look at My hands." And He showed them His hands and they had MARKS on them from the nails! Then He showed them His feet. There were MORE nail marks! IT WAS REALLY JESUS!

And as if THAT weren't enough to prove it, He stayed there and ate supper with them!

That was the first, the very first, the very FIRST EVER Easter in all the world!

And it all happened because God loves us. And He wants us to be members of His family!

ALLELUIA!

Snacks

Snack Tips

In addition to keeping kids' faces smiling and their tummies full, snacks can also provide an enriching learning experience: kids get a chance to learn cooperation, sharing and how things are measured and food is actually prepared. Many of the recipes can be used to help kids experience one of the real joys of showing love to God—preparing something to give to someone else (another group of children, a family member, a shut-in).

The following hints should help make snack time easy, fun and safe for everyone.

Preparation and Organization

When planning to cook, preparation and organization are very important. Before you try recipes that require extensive measuring, it's wise to provide several measuring experiences, showing the children the correct way to use both dry and liquid measuring utensils.

- Provide a comfortable working space that is child-sized.
- Gather and set out ingredients and equipment before children begin.
- Read through the recipe together.
- Go over safety rules together.
- Clean up as you go along.

Safety and Health

- Always wash hands before handling food.
- Things that are hot don't always look hot. If someone gets burned, immediately hold the burned area under cold running water.
- When chopping, cutting or peeling food, use a cutting board.
- Keep pot handles on the stove turned away from you.
- Turn the burner or oven off before removing pans.

- Stand mixing bowls in the sink to avoid splashes as you stir.
- Use hand beaters, a large spoon or a wire whisk instead of electric beaters. This way, children have a chance to get the feel of the batter.
- Demonstrate and let children practice using utensils.
- Store sharp utensils out of children's reach.
- Keep hands dry while working in the kitchen. Wet, slippery hands can cause spills and accidents.
- Keep pot holders dry. If damp, they will absorb heat and lead to burns.

- When cutting with a knife, always cut away from yourself and keep fingers away from the blade.
- To help prevent steam burns, tip the lid away from you whenever you raise the cover of a hot pan.
- Electrical appliances should be used by ADULTS ONLY.

- Young children should not use the stove at all.
- Make sure hot foods are thoroughly cooked and any leftovers are quickly refrigerated.
- Instruct children in advance how to deal with a sneeze or a cough.

(These helpful cooking tips are from *The Big Book of Theme Parties, Snacks and Games* from Gospel Light.)

Popcorn Mix

Materials: 2 tablespoons butter, 2 table-spoons honey, 4 cups popped popcorn, 4 cups Bran Chex, 1 8-ounce package dried apricots, knife, small bowl, electric frying pan, wooden spoon, measuring cup and spoons, small Styrofoam cups or small paper plates.

Preparation: Cut up dried apricots and place in bowl. Set out all materials so that children can see ingredients.

Procedure: With adult supervision, children melt butter in frying pan and stir in honey. Children add popcorn and Chex and stir mixture well. Toast at 250° for 15 to 20 minutes, stirring occasionally. Add apricots before serving in Styrofoam cups or on paper plates. Yield: 12-16 servings.

Spring Punch

Materials: 3 cups strawberries, 2 bottles apple juice, 2 bottles lemon-lime soda, knife, blender or food processor, measuring cup, mixing spoon, punch bowl, serving ladle and cups.

Preparation: Clean strawberries and remove leafy tops. Puree strawberries in blender or food processor. Set out all materials so that children can see ingredients.

Procedure: Children mix pureed strawberries, apple juice and lemon-lime soda in punch bowl. Ladle into cups and serve.

pureed strawberries

Peanut Butter Banana Balls

Materials: 2 1/4 cups graham cracker crumbs, 1/2 cup peanut butter, 1 ripe banana, plate, small bowl, fork, large bowl, measuring cups, large spoon, small paper plates.

Preparation: Pour 1/4 cup graham cracker crumbs on plate. Set out all materials so that children can see ingredients.

Procedure: Have one child peel the banana and break it into pieces in small bowl. Children take turns mashing banana with fork. Measure out 1/2 cup mashed banana. In large bowl, children stir together 2 cups of the crumbs, the peanut butter and the banana. Children take turns to knead mixture with hands until well blended. Children shape spoonfuls of mixture into 1-inch (2.5-cm) balls and roll balls in graham cracker crumbs on plate. Children place their completed balls on paper plates. Yield: about 3 dozen.

Popcorn Shapes

Materials: 2 to 3 quarts popped popcorn, 2 tablespoons butter, 12 large marshmallows, shortening or butter, large resealable plastic bags, rolling pins, large bowl, saucepan, hot plate or stove, measuring spoon, wooden spoon, metal cookie cutters with high sides, waxed paper, paper plates.

Preparation: Place some popcorn into each plastic bag. Set out all materials so that children can see ingredients.

Procedure: Children crush the popcorn using rolling pins and place crushed popcorn in large bowl. With adult supervision, children melt butter in saucepan and then add marshmallows, stirring until marshmallows are melted and well blended with butter. Children pour mixture over crushed popcorn and mix thoroughly. Allow mixture to cool slightly. Children use shortening or butter to lightly grease cookie cutters and then place greased cookie cutters on waxed paper. Children firmly pack the popcorn-marshmallow mixture into each cutter. After each cutter is packed, children carefully remove the cutters and let shapes harden before serving on paper plates.

Fruit Pizza

Materials: 2 1/3 cup buttermilk baking mix, 1/2 cup milk, 4 tablespoons sugar, 3 tablespoons melted butter or margarine, 1 8-ounce package of cream cheese, 1/2 teaspoon vanilla, a variety of fresh fruits (bananas, apples, peaches, nectarines, oranges, kiwi fruit, etc.) or canned fruits (after draining off the liquid), stove, oven mitt, small saucepan, measuring cups and spoons, large bowls, mixing spoon, pizza pan, knives, cutting boards, paper plates; optional—2/3 cup sugar, 2 tablespoons cornstarch, 1/4 teaspoon salt, 1 cup orange juice, saucepan.

Preparation: Melt butter or margarine in saucepan. In large bowl, mix baking mix, milk, 3 tablespoons sugar and butter or margarine to form a soft dough. Spread the dough evenly to the edges of a round, ungreased pizza pan. Bake for 10 to 15 minutes at 425°. Cool. Set out cream cheese at room temperature to soften. Set out all materials so that children can see all ingredients.

Procedure: Children combine softened cream cheese, 1 tablespoon sugar and vanilla in a bowl and mix until well blended. Children spread cream cheese mixture over pizza crust. Children slice a variety of fruits and place the slices on the cheese mixture. Slice pizza edge to edge across the middle 8 times and serve slices on paper plates. Yield: 16 servings.

(Optional: Make a glaze for the fruit pizza by combining 2/3 cup sugar with 2 tablespoons cornstarch, 1/4 teaspoon salt and 1 cup orange juice in a saucepan. Boil the mixture for 1 minute. Cool for 5 minutes before spreading over fruit.)

Animal Cutout Sandwiches

Materials: 1/2 pound butter, 1 large loaf soft bread, 1 16-ounce package processed cheese slices, bread knives, paper plates, large animal-shaped cookie cutters

Preparation: Set out butter at room temperature to soften. Set out all materials so that children can see ingredients.

Procedure: Each child butters two slices of bread and then places cheese slice between bread slices. Child places sandwich on paper plate and uses cookie cutter to cut animal shape out of sandwich.

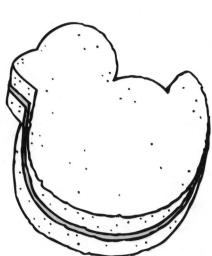

Matzos and Hard-Boiled Eggs

Materials: 8 eggs, 2 cups whole wheat flour and extra flour for dusting hands, oil, water, small pot, stove, oven mitt, salt, baking sheet, measuring cup, small glass bowl, large bowl, mixing spoon, rolling pins, waxed paper, fork, paper plates.

Preparation: Hard-boil eggs in small pot of water. Grease baking sheet with oil. Set out all materials so that children can see ingredients.

Procedure: In large bowl, children mix flour with 1/2 to 3/4 cup water to form dough. Dust lightly with flour. Children flour hands and take turns to knead dough for 3 to 5 minutes. Divide dough into 6 to 8 balls. Children press balls flat with hands and then roll to 1/8-inch (.3125-cm) thickness on waxed paper. Children place matzos on oiled baking sheet, prick with fork and sprinkle with salt. Bake 8 to 10 minutes in 450° oven. Matzos can be eaten while soft or may be left to become crisp in oven once it has been turned off. Place finished matzos on paper plates. Children mix salt with water in glass bowl and then peel and eat eggs dipped in salt water along with the matzos. Yield: 8 servings.

salt

water

eggs

Cinnamon Yogurt

Materials: 1/2 pound vanilla yogurt, 1 teaspoon ground cinnamon, 1-1 1/2 teaspoons honey, mixing bowl and spoon, measuring spoons, melba toast or stoned wheat crackers, knives, paper plates.

Preparation: Set out all materials so that children can see ingredients.

Procedure: Children take turns mixing yogurt with cinnamon and honey in bowl, mixing until smooth. Children spread mixture on toast or crackers and serve on paper plates. Yield: 6-8 servings.

Pita Bread

Materials: 6 whole wheat pita bread halves, cream cheese, 1 6-ounce can pitted black olives, knives, cutting boards, paper plates.

Preparation: Set out cream cheese at room temperature to soften. Set out all materials so that children can see ingredients.

Procedure: On cutting boards, children cut pita bread halves into halves again to make triangles. Children spread cream cheese inside the pita triangles. Children chop olives and sprinkle them on cream cheese. Serve on paper plates. Yield: 12 servings.

cream cheese

pita bread

chopped olives

Nana 'n' Cookie Pudding

Materials: 6 ripe bananas, 2 6-ounce packages vanilla instant pudding, milk, 1 12-ounce box vanilla wafers, 1 8-ounce container non-dairy dessert topping, 1 7-ounce package flaked coconut, resealable plastic bags, knives, cutting boards, measuring cup, stove, mixing bowl and spoon, ladle, rolling pins, clear plastic cups (or small Styrofoam cups), spoons.

Preparation: Place several wafers in each plastic bag. Set out dessert topping at room temperature to thaw. Set out all materials so that children can see ingredients.

Procedure: Children peel and, on cutting boards, cut bananas into slices. With adult supervision, children make pudding according to package directions. Let pudding stand five minutes. Using rolling pins, children crush wafers in plastic bags and place layer of crushed cookies into bottoms of cups. Next, they spoon some of the pudding over the wafers and arrange banana slices over the pudding. Children then top with dessert topping and shredded coconut. Provide spoons when pudding cups are completed and ready to eat. Yield: 10-12 servings.

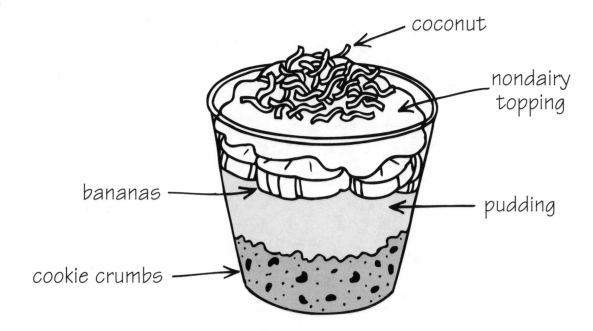

coconut

nondairy topping

bananas

pudding

cookie crumbs

Soft Pretzels

Materials: 1 1/2 cups warm water and some extra water for brushing on baked shapes, 1 package yeast, 1 teaspoon salt, 1 tablespoon sugar, 4 cups flour, 1 egg, shortening, course salt, cookie sheets, small bowl, fork or whisk, stove, oven mitt, large mixing bowl, mixing spoon, measuring cups and spoons, pastry brush, napkins.

Preparation: Grease cookie sheets with shortening. In a small bowl, beat egg with fork or whisk. Set out all materials so that children can see ingredients.

Procedure: Preheat oven to 425°. With adult supervision, children warm water on stove and then pour water into large mixing bowl. Children sprinkle yeast on water and stir until dissolved. Children add salt, sugar and flour to bowl and mix to form dough. Children take turns to knead dough. Each child rolls small ball of dough into a thin rope and then shapes rope into a pretzel, a letter, a numeral or some other shape. Children lay shapes on cookie sheets and brush shapes with beaten egg. Bake for 12 to 15 minutes. After shapes have cooled, children brush shapes with small amount of water and sprinkle with salt. Use napkins for serving. Yield: 10-12 servings.

Chow Mein Chewies

Materials: 1 12-ounce package butterscotch pieces, 1/2 cup peanut butter, 1 6-ounce can chow mein noodles, 1 cup peanuts, cookie sheet, waxed paper, measuring cups, large saucepan, hot plate or stove, wooden spoon, spoons, napkins.

Preparation: Line cookie sheet with waxed paper. Set out all materials so that children can see ingredients.

Procedure: With adult supervision, children place butterscotch pieces and peanut butter in saucepan. Children cook mixture over low heat until butterscotch pieces and peanut butter have melted. Children remove saucepan from heat. Children add noodles and peanuts and stir well. Children drop spoonfuls of mixture onto waxed paper and let stand until firm. Once chewies have set, serve with napkins. Yield: 10-12 servings.

Fresh Fruit with Coconut Dip

Materials: A variety of fruit (watermelon, cantaloupe, papaya, mangoes, tangerines, oranges, apples, strawberries, bananas, etc.), 1/2 cup chopped peanuts, 1 small can frozen lemonade, 1 cup coconut cream (available in gourmet markets and health food stores), cutting boards, knives, measuring cup, serving plate, mixing bowl and spoon, small bowls, toothpicks, napkins.

Preparation: Set out lemonade at room temperature to thaw. Set out all materials so that children can see ingredients.

Procedure: Children peel and, on cutting boards, cut the fruit into small pieces. Children arrange the fruit on serving plate and sprinkle with chopped peanuts. To make the dip, children mix the lemonade and coconut cream in bowl and stir until lemonade and cream are thoroughly combined. Put dip into small bowls. Children use toothpicks to dip fruit into dip. Napkins held under the dipped fruit will help catch drips. Yield: about 12 servings.

Australian Lamingtons

Materials: 9x13-inch (22.5x32.5-cm) unfrosted yellow cake, 3 cups powered sugar, 1/3 cup cocoa, 1/2 cup water, 3 tablespoons butter or margarine (melted), 3 cups shredded coconut, knife, bowl, small pot, hotplate or stove, small saucepan, large saucepan, mixing bowl and spoon, pie tin, wire rack, forks, paper plates; optional—mixing bowl, green food coloring, 1 package of small jellybeans.

Preparation: Cut cake into 2-inch (5-cm) cubes. Set out all materials so that children can see ingredients.

Procedure:

Children mix sugar and cocoa in a bowl. With adult supervision, children melt butter in small saucepan and set aside.

Children boil water in small pot. Children add boiling water and melted butter to sugar and cocoa mixture in bowl and mix until well combined and smooth. To keep bowl of icing warm, children set it in large

hot water

saucepan about one-fourth full of simmering water. Children place coconut in a pie tin next to the saucepan. (Optional: In a mixing bowl, stir several drops of green food coloring into the coconut to make it green. Then place coconut in pie tin.) Children place a wire rack on the other side of the coconut, in assembly-line fashion.

Using forks, children dip each square of cake into the warm icing and let the excess icing drip off. Then they

coconut

roll iced cake in coconut on all sides and place on wire rack to cool. (Optional: After cake is covered with the coconut, children may place a few jelly beans on the top of each cake. If you have colored the coconut green, the jelly beans will resemble Easter eggs hidden in grass.) Serve cooled Lamingtons on paper plates. Yield: 12-15 servings.

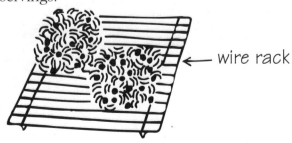

wire rack